My Empire in Social Media

Speaking in International Conference on Environment

Leading Delegation to Department of Homeland Security, US

My Empire in Social Media

A Collection of Amazing Range

N.K. Tripathi

GYAN

Published, 2022

Published by

Gyan Publishing House
5, Ansari Road
Daryaganj, New Delhi-110002
Phone: 011-47034999, 9811692060
www.gyanbooks.com
E-mail: books@gyanbooks.com

Printed at: Gyan Press, Delhi.

Cataloging in Publication Data--DK

Courtesy: D.K. Agencies (P) Ltd. <docinfo@dkagencies.com>

Tripathi, Narendra Kumar, author.

My empire in social media : a collection of amazing range & = Sośala mīḍiyā meṃ merā sāmrājya : vismayakārī vividhatā kā saṅgraha / N.K. Tripathi.

pages cm

English and Hindi.

ISBN 9788121220477 (HB)

1. India--History. 2. India--Politics and government. 3. India--Social conditions. 4. Tripathi, Narendra Kumar. I. Title. II. Title: Sośala mīḍiyā meṃ merā sāmrājya : vismayakārī vividhatā kā saṅgraha.

LCC DS436.T75 2021 | DDC 954 23

Dedicated

to

my beloved mother

Late Kamla

(1922-2011)

Contents

Preface

Great physicist Stephen Hawking remarked, "The greatest enemy of knowledge is not ignorance. It is the illusion of knowledge." Nothing illustrates this better than the information put on the social media in recent years. In spite of this illusion in this digital world, the social media has come to stay with us. As a tool it has brought about a revolutionary change in our ability and reach to communicate anything under the sun, at times unmindful of its consequences. I have used this platform to vent my ideas and experiences about many things and places I came across and as I perceived them. I have tried to do it sincerely and candidly.

This book is a collection of my write-ups in the social media. This book is the expression of a person trying to be observant in life in its various facets. It needs no clairvoyance to see that this book is neither mono-thematic nor it is focused on one sphere of human life. Markedly my comments are on different subjects.

Perennial journey is a quintessential part of my life. In childhood I moved with my family. Later my job entailed constant shifting from one place to other. I got the opportunities to closely interact with the poorest of the poor. On the other hand I have watched at close range those who control wealth and power. I have intimately seen exemplary kindness as well as mindless violence. My journey took me to jungles, villages and metros in India and abroad. More important than physical movement was my long journey in the realm of thinking. My comments on anything which affects the people, have an echo of my experiences of this journey. I foresee any social progress or reform in future as a journey. In a way, we all are more concerned with the journey than with the destination.

My main concern has been the issues which directly impact the society, my country and, at times, all mankind. There has been so much of hype and noise on these issues, but I have tried to filter out relevant points. Politics, economy and social matters keep on coming in the write-ups. Politics encompasses all other issues and it is in politics that we search our salvation from all our woes. I have not refrained from commenting on political parties and electoral politics. Caste and gender issues are not honestly addressed by the political class. It is occasional judicial pronouncement which nudges the government to take some positive steps for social reforms. The dignity and equality of women have been mired in communal and political controversies. Unfortunately social media has sharply polarised not only political class, but entire thinking population. This has diminished the country's capacity to find a way forward.

The last decade had been dismal for our economy. After the global recession of 2008, India withstood its shock. Soon after that India lost the animal spirit for economic reforms and paid heavily for political and bureaucratic misdemeanor. Modi promised a lot but could not deliver what we expected. He succumbed to populism and enforced enigmatic demonetisation. I have relentlessly emphasised in favour of economic reforms. Farmers' issues have also been properly addressed in the book. I have tried to suggest a paradigm for viewing politics that will be meaningful to everyone including policy makers. I am aware that no paradigm is eternally valid; nevertheless my effort is to provide a sight which can lead us to our all-round development in near future.

Any critical appreciation of our polity will take us to the scrutiny of our constitutional and other institutions. The health of our state depends upon these institutions. In the book there are write-ups about our legislature and judiciary. I have been critical of our judicial system and functioning of parliament. There is much concern shown to the criminal justice system, which is dilatory, inefficient and incapable of delivering real justice. In this context, I have discussed the police and policing. There are references to our feudal bureaucracy which is unable to see new challenges. Our military is not given due recognition by politicians and bureaucrats. Attention has also been drawn to our inefficacious educational system and environmental issues. There may be repetitions of the subjects but each write up has different issue. I have given substance of some remarkable books. This is not in nature of book review or critical appreciation, but I have tried to give the essence of these books. These are the masterpieces which I read in recent years. The subjects are varied like literature, history, prehistory, epics, mathematics and economic affairs. The writings have been edited, wherever needed. At the end of every write up, the date of the post in social media is given to appreciate the context. I have included a few writings which I wrote during my university life and I have posted them now on social media. The book takes you to some places in India and abroad, which I visited in last few years. Travelling to different places fills my mind and heart with enthusiasm for life. All the pictures of these places are from my mobile phone.

Social media walks with long strides and is always rushing against the time. At the same time, it is for us to probe a bit deeper and to be conscious that logic can be patient, for it is eternal. I am sure that there will be some ideas in the book which will glimmer in the mind of the reader to reflect for them.

Chapter- 1

From Here and There

Art of Forwarding

The social media, riding over internet, has pervaded the entire social and intellectual discourse. WhatsApp has 1.5 billion users and slightly lesser number use Facebook. We also have clientele for many other platforms. They are all communicating and generating messages. Barring a few posts of personal nature, most of the communication is on wide variety of subjects. The purpose is to stay in touch with known or unknown friends and pass time with recreation and probably knowledge.

Very few persons post the original contents on social media. A vast majority of users simply forward the messages according to their choice or inclination. Some people routinely forward 'good morning' messages, flowers or pictures of Gods and Goddesses. Some specialise in forwarding only the jokes. Some give you words of wisdom or sermons which sound great but have little substance. Some are politically motivated, mostly with one polarised track, and their posts are at times very pungent and vicious. Some surprise you with action packed wonders or acrobatics. Some choose their forward from a very wide spectrum from art to health issues. Some try to surprise or impress you with more and more unique posts.

Sometimes messages are forwarded without application of any mind. We mechanically forward things (or like them) on WhatsApp or fb. Once I saw a message which stated that in this February there are exact 4 weeks starting from Monday. This February, they falsely claimed, will not come in your life as it comes once in 843 years and calling it money bags. Actually such February is far more frequent.

Some generate fake news with ulterior motives and pass it furtively. Many gullible start forwarding believing them to be true. This can be dangerous at times for law and order. WhatsApp is now labelling its forwarded messages in a move that the company hopes will curb some of the app's viral misinformation problems. In a blog post published earlier today, WhatsApp announced the new label, which will indicate that a message has been forwarded to someone from other user.

Social media has poured so much of information that human brains are torn to the brim. Intellectual curiosity has been replaced with search for more and more sensational trash. Originality has taken a back seat.

Forwarding has become a fine art. People read many messages from different sources, selecting according to their taste they pass on to others. Most of the times, you can see the same message at different places. May be forwarding has become an art with many genres for long time to come, till a more disruptive technology takes over.

Salute to forwarders!

9 May, 2019

Environment

We as human beings are too occupied in our daily chores or at the most in local or national activities. We fail to see a long term vista of survival and development of mankind. The preservation of environment is one such important issue. Our Janparishad is organising an International Conference (contact www.eaunsdg.com) in Bhopal on this subject on 17-19/12/2016.

As chairman of this organisation, I express my views for this conference as under:-

> It is a great sense of pride and achievement for Janparishad that it has successfully organised three International Conferences. Now as a next step in our forward march we are organising Fourth International Conference on Environment and Agriculture in UN Sustainable Development Goals. The UN has declared 17 sustainable development goals (SDGs) and as many as six of them are directly related to environment and agriculture but eventually all goals are about the type of the development which will ensure a safe and clean planet forever. We have to provide and sustain supply of water and food for all. We have to ensure economic growth with green energy. The mankind will be best advised to conserve and sustainably use the oceans, marine resources and terrestrial ecosystems. Finally we have to combat climate change. We can feel relieved with the requisite support of the international community by the declaration of 2015 Paris Climate Conference (COP 21).

This fourth International Conference will focus on identifying the issues which relate to environment and agriculture for sustainable development goals. This will suggest new innovations in agriculture. We will encourage the participants of the Conference to propound their own plans and ideas for the realisation of these declared goals. The conference will aim for inculcating positive attitudes among young generation towards these crucial issues which are significant for the survival of the life on this earth.

I am personally very grateful to the Government of Madhya Pradesh for providing assistance through EPCO in organising this event. Sustainability Transition Consulting, Austin, USA (SusTranCon), has once again extended whole hearted support to us.

17 December, 2016

Birth of Responsible Social Media

I attended a graceful and meaningful function for the inauguration of the portal of Mediawala, organised today at Hotel Jehan Numa, Bhopal. It was inaugurated by my old friend Shri O P Rawat, who is presently Chief Election Commissioner of India. The portal is launched by Ex-Director, Public Relations MP, Shri Suresh Tiwari and Journalist Shri Prakash Hindustani who deserve appreciation.

It was a remarkable programme because of high level of talks by eminent speakers on a topic of utmost importance. The topic was 'Election, Public Opinion and Social Media'. Mr Manoj Shrivastav, IAS threw light on international experiences and concerns of different democratic countries. In Indian context old malpractices of election like paid news are now becoming irrelevant in view of the far more effective manipulation of social media. Big social media giants like Facebook have devised such algorithms which can read into the psyche of potential voters, after which it will be possible to micro manage the electoral manipulation. Western democracies have realised the threat from Russia and organisations like Cambridge Analytica. Senior journalists who were invited as speakers contributed their views on the topic from different aspects.

Chief guest Shri OP Rawat, CEC spoke about the role of Election Commission and future challenges in Indian context.

Mediawala, with which I am associated, has pledged for honest reporting.

10 April, 2018

Exercises for Quality Life

There is a well-known cliché 'a sound mind is found in a healthy body'. This is true.

To keep body in efficient functioning, it requires regular exercises for every person especially elderly men and women. The body should respond to all challenges effortlessly and painlessly. For advancing age, exercise is essential. Elderly people fortunately have more time available at their disposal.

Unfortunately no one single exercise (including walking) is enough for wellness. It has to be a combination of different types of exercises with appropriate frequencies. I provide here a brief account from my own personal study and experience:-

1. *Brisk Walking daily:-* it is one of the best aerobic exercises. Brisk walk should begin and end slowly. In severe pollution and cold weather conditions, one can use treadmill, cycle or cross trainer.
2. *Flexibility thrice a week:-* stretching or some Yoga exercises.
3. *Strength twice a week:-* resistance, gym, callisthenics, dumbbells, bands etc.
4. *Balance thrice a week:-* tandem and reverse walk, standing on one leg, walking on toes and heels etc.

5. *Breathing exercise daily:-* any type of breathing exercise or short pranayam.

All these exercises are required for all persons of all ages and both sexes. Finally keep your mind always fresh and stress free by avoiding negative thoughts and seeing life in a positive perspective. Be physically and mentally healthy and enjoy the world.

Start exercise today!

11 July, 2019

Sleeping in Open: Old Times

In this picture what you see, was to give an experience for a night to my granddaughters. They were very keen to sleep outside after learning from me that for most of my early life, like others in those days, I used to sleep in open during summers and, if it was not raining, also during monsoon. They never knew such thing, until I told them in this lockdown.

Let me remind the present young millennial generation that there were times when people in cities and towns slept outside during warm nights. People used to sleep in courtyard, veranda, terrace or any other open space. Fans were not available in all the rooms in most of the houses, not to talk of coolers and ACs. We all slept on old-fashioned cots called *charpai* or *khatia*. Only a few people used mosquito nets tied on bamboos and cross- fixed in the legs of the cots.

My excited granddaughters got a feel of sleeping out last night.

25 July, 2020

Rameshwaram Conch

While cleaning my small little temple for Diwali, I noticed the date on this Conch Shell. It is 14-7-1975. It was taken from Rameshwaram as souvenir during Bharat Darshan, while we were doing our basic training of IPS. Rameshwaram temple is dedicated to God Shiva located on an island in Tamil Nadu. It is one of the most venerated temples, and is one of the four Dhams and twelve Jyotirlinga temples.

I felt nostalgic with this 44 years old piece.

20 October, 2019

Wushu in Brunei

Last year on these dates, I and my wife had gone as observers of Indian Wushu (martial art) team in 10th Asian Junior Championship being held at Brunei. The Championship was opened on 19-8-2019. The team was photographed with the Indian Ambassador in Brunei, Mr Ajnish Kumar. On his left are me and my wife Laxmi.

Brunei is a beautiful tiny country in Southeast Asia. We got a chance to see its magnificent mosques, hotels and dense rainforest.

20 August, 2020

With Lions

Lions have always captured the imagination of men. The earliest depiction found is dating back to about 32,000 years ago during Palaeolithic period in the cave art of Chauvet, France. Lions had been part of Ancient Egyptian, Greek, and Indian civilisations. Sphinx dating back 4,600 years still stands in Egypt before the pyramids. Many Greek stories are around lions. Indian mythology depicts most venerated Devi Durga proudly riding a lion. The historic pillar of Ashok the Great, has four lions facing four directions, symbolising power, courage, confidence and pride.

13 September, 2018

Reorientation Course in Ludo

Most of us must have played Ludo and Snakes and Ladders in our childhood. Along with carom board, these indoor games were considered elite and a good pastime during summer vacations. For outdoor, we had kabaddi, gulli dunda and makeshift cricket.

This lockdown imposed by Modi has provided a fresh experience of togetherness among family members. Because of the facility of work from home for my daughter and the holidays of my granddaughters, they joined us just before the lockdown. My granddaughters, especially younger one, treat me like a child. She should have my undivided attention to her all the time. I attend from some distance her online classes (class II). After over half a century, I have been trained again in ludo and snakes and ladders and I devote considerable time for this activity. I also learnt a new game called 'treasure hunt' in which treasure is hunted by clues hidden somewhere in the rooms.

She has stopped my watching TV news and debates. I am permitted to see only family viewing of Ramayana and Mahabharata. If I try to see news, it is changed to some strange cartoons. My book and news paper are snatched and pushed aside. I have to be part of videos where she pretends like a TV reporter to tell us about precautions to be taken for Corona. She can make fun of me in many manners. Pony tail is tried on my leftover hair. My wife's dhoti is wrapped around me to laugh at me. The only serious discussion with her is after dinner on my side-terrace about the prominent stars and planets visible in the sky.

I have no time to think about the mundane things like future of India during lockdown.

4 May, 2020

News From Far-off

On 25th, December the PM Modi inaugurated the Bogibeel Bridge on the mighty river Brahmaputra in Assam. Our mainstream media, highly intoxicated with politics, mentioned this bridge with somewhat indifference.

However, for me it was real life news. I had spent one year in Assam during infamous and violent Assam Agitation. I had to travel all over the state braving poor connectivity. To avoid long distances I had to cross Brahmaputra (of course not during monsoon) with my vehicle in big boats in places like Nimati Ghat. Many bridges have come up in Assam since then, but the latest is a big situation changer.

The Bogibeel Bridge, inside Assam, is 20 km from the border of Arunachal Pradesh. It connects Dibrugarh on the Brahmaputra's south bank to Dhemaji on the north bank. While railway lines run along both the banks, a train crossing on the Brahmaputra was possible at only two places. Both these rail and road options, one in Jogighopa in western Assam and other on the outskirts of Guwahati (Saraighat Bridge) are hundreds of kilometres from the eastern Assam-Arunachal border. Both existing bridges bring trains from the north bank to Guwahati on the south. The Bogibeel Bridge provides an alternative in the east. This will also help in easy movement of armed forces between the left and the right banks of the river.

Within the Northeast, the train journey between Assam and Arunachal Pradesh is now reduced from 500 km to 100 km, according to details released by the project developers. So far, travellers had to make the loop via Guwahati. For the rest of India too, Dibrugarh becomes more accessible without travelling via Guwahati. The train journey from Delhi to Dibrugarh is reduced by 3 hours (from 37 hours to 34) and the distance by 170 km.

North-east is still waiting for a nearly 20 km long bridge over Brahmaputra connecting Dhubri in lower Assam and Phulbari in Meghalaya. It may be ready by 2027.

30 December, 2018

Passing Three Lockdowns

Three Lockdowns have finished today with over 90 thousand Covid-19 cases. It is time for me to take a stock of my own well-being. It was a difficult confinement period for me, as I am a person who doesn't stay in one city for more than a few weeks.

Bombardment of corona statistics and details of disease, medicine and probable vaccines filled the mind space. Therefore, we were all advised from the day one to take care of our physical and mental well-being. I took it rather seriously.

My physical activities continued as there was no disruption. For aerobic, there was walking inside the house and the cycling. Stretching and breathing exercises were also daily affairs. Strength and balance exercises were done periodically. There was no disturbance and, more importantly, there was no threat of disturbance. The mind got many preoccupations. While some stressed, some worked as de-stressing. In the beginning for a fortnight, it was my detoxification period away from the social media. Mahabharat and Ramayan serials watched by whole family kept me away from meaningless TV debates. Some amount of time was taken by online official work and monitoring of the patients in our university hospital. I toyed with the idea of my possible book.

However, the largest part of my time was taken away by my granddaughter which was also the time for stress elimination. It included many little games for which I regained my expertise. After dinner, it was the finest time to take a stroll on terrace. This was the time to arouse the curiosity in me and my granddaughter for the moon, stars, clouds and breeze.

If necessary, I am ready to face more lockdowns.

17 May, 2020

With Young Lions in Gwalior

A Feel to Granddaughters for Sleeping in Open

Chapter - 2

Revealing Social Imperitives

Women of India

Women of India! beware and be cautious of the religious preachers. They are called Baba, Sant, Muni, Maulvi, Bishop and Godman etc. They all have one thing in common. They see everything in this world through the eyes of men. Their all teachings of behaviour and morality are for women. They will tell women to be obedient to everyone. For them women have no individuality or personality of their own. She has to always serve someone.

We are in 21st century in which all right thinking people talk about complete equality of all human beings. I think women are also human beings and should be allowed to think for themselves and should not be given sermons.

I think more and better education will take women in the direction of ethical justice.

22 August, 2015

Pink- A bold and daring Movie

Pink is an unusually exploring picture into the present day Indian society and its contradictions and hypocrisies.

An emerging and aspirational middle class has produced a large number of courageous and intelligent girls in metros and other cities. These girls want social equality with boys. This alarms a deeply conservative section which also claims to be the custodian of Indian culture. This section of society is also hypocrite.

I belong to a generation which in its youth was not supposed to even look at girls, forget about talking to them. My old generation is now confused with our present day youth. We have to have a modern outlook. Our boys are nurtured with a mindset of our chauvinistic atmosphere. When our girls interact freely with boys, then the old traditionalists think that youth is taking liberty with morals. It is not seen in this way in any other developed societies of the world.

This movie is a great effort to shake our traditional ideas. Congratulations Pink !!

20 September, 2016

Triple Talaq and Secularism

To avoid any ambiguity, the Indian Constitution was specifically declared secular in 1976 by 42nd amendment. So our country is secular and that ideally means that state will keep away from religion. Secularism in European context means separation of the state and the church. However, in India, we are a nation obsessed with religion, not only in our private faith but unfortunately in all social and political spheres. Even the constitution bench for Triple Talaq comprises of Judges of all religions so that it looks secular.

Recently nation heard two topmost advocates. Harish Salve was brilliant in International Court of Justice whereas Kapil Sibbal argued like a conservative in the Supreme Court. Talking about the Triple Talaq, he said that it should continue just because it is being practiced for last 1400 years. He meant that we should follow everything which is a custom. No new ideas, no new logical practice, no innovation of science should be accepted because all these are not customary. It is of no concern to Kapil Sibbal that great prophet Muhammad himself stopped or changed many of the old Arabian bad practices prevailing in his time.

Article 14 of the constitution is the soul of all fundamental rights. It gives right to equality and this means that everyone is equal before law. So women are equal to men in law. Article 25 allows everyone to practice his/her religion. Kapil Sibbal argues that Muslim men are well within their rights to practice Triple Talaq as it is part of their religion. By implication women have only the right to suffer!

India has many religions and they all have or had many discriminatory customs against women. Many of them have been abolished but still much has to be done. In Triple Talaq case, the SC has to decide the meeting point of the Articles 14 and 25. While many Islamic countries have abolished this practice, secular India is struggling after 70 years of independence to concede rights to women to be equal to men.

19 May, 2017

Karwa Chauth

Karwa Chauth is a fast for Hindu married women to ensure long and prosperous lives of their husbands. There are some more occasions to fast for such Suhagins (having husbands) to achieve similar fortunes. There is not a single day in a year or in whole life of men for any reciprocal rituals. A news item today in TOI says that Karwa Chauth is on decline in metros among couples. Young husbands with modern conscience are requesting their wives to abandon this fast. This also shows the rise of modern and educated working women.

All the rituals, restrictions and traditions are mostly for women in all religions and Karwa Chauth is no exception. This so called festival totally subjugates women to misogynistic world view of men. Those who favour the end of triple talaq should also give a thought to it.

8 October, 2017

Girl Child's Sexual Abuse and Society

(Organised by INDORE PRESS CLUB)

Indore Press Club organised a brainstorming session yesterday on an important but sad issue of sexual abuse of girl child. It was organised in collaboration with an organisation, Seva Surabhi. The most enlightened and socially spirited citizens of Indore participated in it. It had men, women, girls and representatives of political parties, MLAs, religious leaders, media, NGOs, police, students and various professionals. I felt honoured to be invited in it to give concluding address.

All speakers focused on the causes of sexual abuse and suggestions to protect '*betian*' (daughters). Overwhelmingly the general tenor of speakers was conservative and traditional. Among various causes of sexual abuse, the speakers emphasised on present day decline of moral values and decay of our old culture. Some criticised the modern dresses, girls going to pubs and getting drunk. Some bold girls however, stood to repudiate such arguments and asserted for equal rights as enjoyed by boys. Some deplored the bad effects of the TV serials in breaking the homes. The rise of new social phenomenon of live-in partnership was also decried. A large number of speakers also blamed the wide spread availability and use of narcotic drugs and requested the police to raid the drug-pedlars. Drawbacks of police and legal system were also highlighted. A few speakers, mainly women and small girls, focused on the main issue of sexual assaults on very small children and gave very useful suggestion of always monitoring the behaviour of girl child and take any change in her behaviour very seriously. One wise lady suggested that parents should not only teach their daughters about good norms but pay more attention to their boys to tell them to respect girls. A lady police officer tried to reconcile various views in a very mature way.

I gave my concluding remarks and warned that for kids we have to be more careful of known persons as almost 90% of sexual abuse cases are committed by either close relatives or so called 'friends' of the family. No case should be hidden in the name of the family reputation. There is also need for continuous sensitisation of police and judges on gender issues.

I congratulate to Indore Press Club for organising a meaningful interaction.

17 July, 2018

#MeToo to #AkbarToo

One year ago Alyssa Milano, a Hollywood actress, posted on Twitter: "If you've been sexually harassed or assaulted write '#me too' as a reply to this tweet." Within 24 hours, she had received more than 5,00,000 responses with the hashtag "#MeToo". Yet the past 12 months appear to have made Americans more cynical about sexual harassment, according to polls conducted for famous magazine, *The Economist*. Interestingly followers of Hillary have far more faith in #MeToo than those of Trump.

In contrast Indian #MeToo is in a real sense only a few days old and already it has evoked bewildering variety of reactions. They range from juicy disdain to typical WhatsApp jokes. Some even called it an insurance policy of now less glamorous old women. Indifferent ones doubt about the inordinate delay of 10, 20 or 30 years in reporting the sexual misconduct. Misogynistic expressions have come from many quarters. However, a large section of enlightened women and a minuscule of men have taken this as a movement to be used for women's safety. #MeToo is basically a movement against sexual misconduct at work place. Atrocities on women inside the house and outside are rampant everywhere and more so in traditional society like India but this movement has a limited scope. #MeToo has become possible because of easy availability of social media with wide audience. It has given courage to many in film industry, legal profession and media where better known women have come out in open. One hopes that in future women from politics as well as from all types of offices will follow the suit. For the present for no other option, we can ignore a vast multitude of poor women whose workplaces are construction sites, fields, brick kilns or domestic four walls.

There are people who are taking a legalistic view of these allegations. They want these complaining women to prove their charges in the court of law. Some of these people are well meaning but a number of these legalists are having a vicarious pleasure of the obvious helplessness of the victims. Lodging FIRs will be very difficult and if at all these cases go to the courts they have to face the hurdle of Section 468 CrPC regarding limitation on action. If the delay is condoned, then these women have to face gruelling cross-examination by the most hostile lawyers who may put most uncivilised questions. Our criminal justice system is quite useless because it is dilatory, expensive and humiliating for victims.

Politicians, it is said, have the least of the conscience and this is doubly proved by a junior minister, MJ Akbar. No less than his 20 junior female journalists came out with complaints of sexual harassment while working under him. It was apparent to a compassionate observer that allegations are genuine. Akbar was most preposterous in suggesting that these women have entered into a conspiracy against him. He bulldozed them by filing criminal defamation under Section 500 IPC. Modi government looked the other way. Only when these women dared to stand judicial scrutiny, the Government panicked and showed Akbar the door.

With years of deep agony, these women with the support of other victims have now come out in open. If for nothing else, it is at least a feeble revenge of naming and shaming, leaving the rest for the society to think. #MeToo is a social movement and depends only on individual and social conscience.

18 October, 2018

Padmavat – Film and Facts

I saw this movie today. This movie was highlighted because of the opposition of Karni Sena against its release. In some places Karni Sena resorted to violence. This gave good publicity to the movie and, in spite of not being a masterpiece, it did good business. In my college days I had read the book Padmavat by the Awadhi poet Malik Muhammad Jayasi.

The film starts with a disclaimer (insisted by CBFC) which says that all characters, places and incidents are imaginary. I think this is reasonable. Yet the overall film is very close to what we had been hearing since childhood and it arouses controversy. First let us be clear about the known history. Delhi Sultan Alauddin Khilji (1296-1316) attacked Chittor fort in 1303 and defeated the king. The poet

Amir Khusro accompanied the Sultan and has given the account of the battle but without giving the name of the Rajput king or any story of Padmavati or Padmini and about Johar. Sultan won the battle and conducted a gruesome mass massacre of about thirty thousand people inside the fort.

The film is based on Malik Mohammad Jayasi's Padmavat. Jayasi himself made it very clear that his story is imaginary. His character Ratan Sen was not of that era and generals Gora and Badal fought much later in 1488 against Ghayasuddin Khilji, the governor of Malwa (not Delhi). The character of Padmavati seems wholly imaginary.

Jayasi wrote this epic which is of very high quality. His patron was a Rajput king and therefore he has praised the Rajput valour. He was a great Sufi poet and in this book he has used allegory for Sufism. Raja Ratan Sen is the soul, Padmavati is the virtue and intelligence of a king, Allauddin is the Illusion (maya) and the Chittor fort is the human body. With this allegory he has sung divine poems. This film has not fully followed Jayasi and has its own changes.

However, coming to present time, I would add that India has to grow mentally and intellectually. We should have the courage to look to historical facts dispassionately. We should debate but not get emotional or violent or play dirty politics with historical facts. Yes, from facts we can derive our own conclusions!

28 January, 2018

Abused Muslim Women

Today TOI brought out a very out spoken article by Shazia Ilmi titled 'No Country For Sharia Courts'. It was a spirited defence of brutalised Muslim women expressing full faith in judiciary to uphold the tenets of the constitution.

She declares the practice of Talaq-e Biddat and Nikah Halala to be clearly un-Islamic and against Quran. I quote her:

'Like all other citizens Indian Muslims follow the Indian Penal Code for all civil and criminal disputes. Why does the narrative of their faith being in peril arise only in matters of family law?'

She praises the sensitivity of the judiciary in interpreting Quran and upholding the constitution. Against this practice, she says 'the multitude of mullahs, imams and qazis, constituting a self anointed club of Islamic scholars representing different schools of Islamic jurisprudence, dish out their own concoction of Islamic justice'.

Congress party stifled the saner judicial conscience by demolishing Shah Bano verdict and thereby instigating the rise of Hindu communalism. This step of Congress lacked conviction and was for only vote banks. Much later, BJP has now emerged as the well wisher of Muslim women in a fake and sham sympathy for them. It gives delight to BJP to attack Muslim clergy by playing up the cause of harassed Muslim women.

Let us have faith in our judiciary, which in spite of many drawbacks has the legal and moral authority to enforce the constitutional rights with even hands.

4 August, 2018

Predicament of Indian Muslims

The verdict of the recent 2019 election had been even more decisive for Modi than that of 2014. Earlier I had discussed the political and caste factors in this election. It is incumbent now to focus on the role of the minority in the election as well as in the body politic in general. The largest minority of India, the Muslims (14.2% in 2011 census) after election, are not perfervid part of the ruling party. They are not even of any reckoning in the opposition either and are left without any leverage in the establishment. MPs belonging to the Muslim community are less in number than their proportion in the population. In large parts of India, the Muslims had been voting tactically by giving their votes to any party or combination which can keep the BJP away from power. Muslims feel frustrated that in spite of their best efforts, even in state like UP where they are sizeable in number, they could not stop the juggernaut of BJP. As a matter of fact the tactical voting of Muslims polarised the Hindus to the big advantage of the BJP. This has left the community in a vexatious position.

India has a truly secular Constitution. However, the secularism of India is vastly different from what it is considered to be in the western democracies. In practice secular and many regional parties have played on the fears of the Muslims and simultaneously also appeased them with swags only to garner their votes. I am tempted here to quote an eminent journalist Saba Naqvi, "Secularism is a fine value. But in practice it has been hollowed out for decades and reduced to mere electoral management that sees Muslims as a herd and then tries to combine their votes with those of another herd".

The so called secular parties have exploited the Muslims as a vote bank, and only fostering the most conservative and obscurantist leadership among the Muslims. This has further kept this community away from the modern ideas. While many Muslim countries of the world have marched ahead with reforms, Indian Muslims were compelled by their clerical leadership to remain regressive in social, educational and economic advancements. The nexus of some political parties and such Muslim leaders withheld the progress of the community. This also unfortunately inculcated a sense of alienation.

But should the Muslim community move into deep despondency for being outside the mainstream of political power? No, they may easily regain their animation. Historically Indian Muslims had been a community with a strong humanitarian outlook compared to their brethren outside India. The soft Sufism flourished in the cradle of this subcontinent. Even though a section of the scholars repeatedly highlights the clashes of the religious communities in the historical context, it fails to see the harmonious blend in the peaceful cultural coexistence. I think the time has come for the Muslim youth to come forward and face all the challenges of the modern time. Modi has tried to reach the Muslim community by declaring 'Sabka Saath Sabka Vikas' and now most importantly 'Sabka Vishwas'. Modi has come out with a programme of five crore scholarships in the next five years for students and especially girls of the minority. He has also announced a scheme of bringing madarsas in line with modern education. Instead of smelling hypocrisy in it, it is time for the Muslims to try and reap advantages in favour of the future of the community. With this enlightenment the Muslims can assert, according to their conscience, politically in different ways other than as a vote bank.

It should be clear to all that the impressive victory of Modi is not the vindication of Hindutva. In Modi's victory there are many genuine secular aspects of new India. The majority community has to find a political equilibrium which enables India to find its rightful place in the world. Again to quote Saba Naqvi who in a sober moment referring to Ram Mandir to be built in Ayodhya and doing away with Article 370 says, "these are culture and identity wars that minorities cannot win. With Amit Shah as home minister many more Muslims would have to prove they are indeed citizens of India. There are reasons to be worried but people cannot live in permanent fear. As individuals they have to work at changing their own life. That is what Fatima cares and she is not afraid".

Like many things in an optimistic life, I can only hope that the state will not transgress the limits of the constitution, and the system will not come in the way of the minority in carving out their way ahead.

12 June, 2019

We Love Violence

India requires occasional violent outlet to remain healthy! It requires the expression of violence today as much as it required in ancient times. Under the peaceful smile of Lord Buddha and solemn chanting of Vedas and Azan, we have seen much bloodshed. Most of this blood did not flow in the battlefields but in our internal internecine conflicts. Seven decades back India became a nation with a constitution over the dead bodies of lakhs of its people, for a cause called partition.

It was expected that after independence India will progress in harmony, with loving fraternity, where violence will have no place and everybody will walk, as Rabindranath Tagore said, 'with his or her head held high'. Alas! Politicians will not allow that to happen. Their minds are petty, their egos are bloated and concerns for others totally missing. No wonder violence is always a part of their policy. Led by such leaders, some people enjoy burning properties. Arson takes out the people's frustrations and their sense of smallness.

Everyone knows in the heart that CAA and NRC are non-issues from the beginning and no person residing in India is ever going to be thrown out of its borders. As regards refugees, in a country of 1.3 billion diverse people, a few of them of any religion hardly matter to it. However, posturing is important. On one side we have a party which is hell bent on consolidating its Hindu vote-bank. For it CAA was only one more reconfirmation of this consolidation. On the other side are various so called liberals of different varieties, some students, political leaders who are left out of the power, and rank communalists. With this division, people get an opportunity to be violent and they love it. The poor police comes in between these two sides. For liberals and the opposition parties the police are always brutal, devoid of any commonsense and inherently sadistic. Surprisingly, mob violence is never condemned by any politician.

Like all turmoil on this sub-continent, this comparatively minor violent phase will also fade away, leaving some scars. After a while, some people will again find another reason for violence.

27 December, 2019

VIP Syndrome

Madras High Court has shocked the conscience of the ordinary citizens of India. Madras High Court, in a surprising order, asks the Central Transport Ministry to ensure that in whole India on all toll barriers separate lanes should be provided for VIP cars including judges' cars. In a country having long entrenched tradition of feudalism, a new breed of VIP culture has taken roots after independence. It is reassuring to recollect that Chief Justice of India was the first person to remove red light of his car, even before the formal orders reached him in this regard.

Why do some privileged people want to assert their authority in public to overawe the poor common man? May be an urge of their psyche compels them to fulfil their traces of feudalism by overtly showing off their so called status. Their inner self is not reconciled to the idea of equality, essential for modern democratic values. We have seen some of our political goons moving in SUVs resorting to violence at toll plazas for being asked to pay or to show their ID.

A few days back I had written about the hooters replacing the red lights on the vehicles of the so called and sometimes fake VIPs. I had requested the transport and traffic departments to take action. They did take some action, not on my asking, but on the instructions of the Election Commission. However, like most of the governmental efforts, this campaign was also half hearted and short lived.

As far as the Madras High Court decision is concerned, I am sure it will be turned down by the Supreme Court.

11 November, 2019

Chapter - 3

Politics is War without Bloodshed

AAP Wins

Congratulations to AAP and Arvind Kejriwal for their spectacular victory in Delhi. I put my brief observations:-

1. This is definitely a victory of the party for its honesty and conviction for the welfare of under privileged. Kejriwal is sincere to what he says.
2. Mr Modi! your arrogance is crushed. Now you better throw your Rs 10 lakh coat in Sabarmati and start working with the simplicity of a chaiwala.
3. Sonia and Rahul Gandhi! you may call a press conference and declare your resignations for ever, before you are removed out by Congressmen.
4. Kejriwal! Delhi is very important, but it is not India. Nation wants fresh breeze of your politics of honesty and commitment for downtrodden and not populism. Good luck.

10 February, 2015

Ramifications of 5 State Elections

I am neither a politician nor a political analyst, however, as a citizen I do think about the happenings in the country.

I will summarise my views on today's results of elections of February - March, 2017 in five states – Uttar Pradesh, Uttarakhand, Punjab, Goa and Manipur:-

- # Modi has emerged as one of the most dominant political leaders in independent India, vehemently admired and equally detested.
- # A section of Indians which is genuinely secular, liberal and inclusive feels frustrated with UP results.
- # In spite of Punjab victory Congress got a body blow in these elections, especially in UP, proving very feeble leadership of Rahul Gandhi. Punjab is won by Amrinder Singh and in spite of the high command. At present Rahul Gandhi is being portrayed as lacking in hard work of 24×7, comprehension and confidence. There is unease among common Congress workers but they don't speak because of the Congress culture.
- # Divine right to rule based on dynasty will not work without hard work. Dynasty without merit in any political party may become a painful liability.
- # There is a crying need for opposition unity to check and balance the frightening power of an emergent BJP. Congress will not easily become the fulcrum of this unity due to its weak leadership. It will equally be difficult for any one regional leader to be accepted by all. Any loose and hasty combination will be thrashed by Modi in 2019.
- # Caste and minority vote banks will not give dividends. In UP trusted vote banks of Muslim, Yadav and Jatav were challenged by all other castes.
- # There is an yearning among people for the transparent and corruption free governance. Demonetisation was

tolerated for this reason. A party must be seen capable of providing such government.

With every passing election, the public becomes more mature.

11 March, 2017

Indian National Congress

I heard Ramchandra Guha in Kolkata on the occasion of Netaji lecture series, talking about the decline of Congress. He is a foremost historian and an ardent admirer of Mahatma Gandhi and Nehru. He is a well wisher of the Congress and opposes the communal ideology of BJP and RSS.

What he said made me sad. He said that the Congress could never again become a big national party. Its decline can only be stopped for a few more years. He approved of the Congress making alliances in Bihar and UP. He also prognosticated that the Congress can only survive for some more years by aligning as junior partner with regional parties. Guha was not optimistic about the role of Rahul Gandhi and claimed that Rahul is not acceptable to a sizeable section of the Congress.

The decline of the Congress will be dangerous for Indian polity since this is the only all inclusive, non-divisive and pan- India party. Only the Congress can keep communal and parochial elements in check. I hope some dynamic and energetic leader from grass root in INC may emerge to take command and lead the liberal and cosmopolitan people of this great nation.

25 January, 2017

Emergency

Emergency was proclaimed on the mid night of 25th June, 1975. Forty two years ago that time I was already in IPS Academy, Hyderabad as trainee. We all trainees were busy in our life little knowing or bothering about what was going on outside in India, least of all about emergency. Newspapers were busy with happy news, like the punctual running of trains.

Mrs Indira Gandhi, the then great PM came to take salute of our final passing out parade and we were all very proud of it.

Once in the district of Khandwa, MP in December, 1975 as probationer I found complete peace in the police working. All troublesome political leaders and criminals were inside Jail under MISA. It was a great time to relax for police.

When finally the results of Lok Sabha came, while I was still in Khandwa in early 1977, the whole nation was stunned by complete wipe out of the grand old party Congress, especially in North India. Surprisingly, Mrs Gandhi lost herself.

In hind sight emergency was a total negation of what our framers of the constitution stood for. All democratic institutions and traditions buckled down under MISA. Most distressing and surprising was the surrender of the committed Judiciary which failed to safeguard the individual freedom.

Fortunately emergency did not pay well to the then ruling party, and therefore this horrid experiment is not likely to be ever repeated by any political party in power in future !

26 June, 2017

Ill-Behaved Netas

Shri Ravindra Gaikwad, MP, Shiv Sena beat one Air India staffer with his sandal for 25 times. This he did due to some presumed provocation. He was debarred by all domestic airlines from air travel. He was largely condemned by public and media. However, the political class, including ruling BJP, timid as they are in such matters, maintained an eerie silence.

Today nation was given a big jolt when parliament found many apologists for this goon. It was fully understandable that Shiv Sena MPs were defending him as they are habitual of resorting to violence and intimidation. It was, however, very surprising that Naresh Agrawal of SP was also defending this rogue. Congress also joined in the chorus of their newly found friend, Samajvadi Party in UP.

MPs are a united class, cutting across political differences, when it comes to saving their perks and privileges. In this they behave like arrogant feudal lords before a meek and poor public kept silent by democracy!

27 March, 2017

Quit India Movement

India celebrates today completion of 75 years of Quit India Movement. Mahatma Gandhi gave a call to compel the Britishers to leave India and he gave a war cry of 'Do or Die'. Congress party and many others inspired by Mahatma joined the agitation and suffered for it.

Today parliament of free India remembered the Movement. Sadly its present leaders are having very narrow and partisan view. Both Modi and Sonia Gandhi disappointed us. Modi exhorted the nation to a vision which his party hardly seems to be striving. Sonia Gandhi primarily attacked the BJP/RSS and claimed complete copyright of the Congress over the movement. She emphasised that RSS did not join the agitation implying therefore they are not fit to rule today.

This is a fact that RSS did not join the movement. But what was not mentioned was that Ambedkar for his own reasons supported the British as he has done throughout the independence struggle. The staunch supporter of the Congress party today, the Left sided with the British. Princely states (some of them now support Congress) opposed the movement. Of course Muslim League also opposed the Congress.

It is to the credit of Mahatma Gandhi that he attracted many people beyond the Congress party including some members from the above mentioned organisations. The Quit India Movement was truly a national uprising.

The British government was able to crush this movement and the movement failed in its immediate objectives. However, the British quit India after five years and we became an independent nation in 1947, albeit with a partitioned map on the ground of religion.

9 August, 2017

Is Modi on Way Out

Modi came as a ray of hope. He promised a clean government with maximum governance. He had something to offer to everyone. He promised economic reforms, high growth and free markets. To the farmers, he promised fair prices of crops. Youth listened to him for new opportunities. He went to every corner of India during election campaign and promised every small region of India its specific economic agenda. He aroused the aspirations of India with promise of 'achchhe din'. No wonder UPA was thrown out with great ease.

Modi started well, but was handicapped by his somewhat timid finance minister and a roadblock of the Rajya Sabha. Congress took full revenge in the Rajya Sabha for BJP's actions during UPA. In the absence of new legislation, Modi came out with a slew of programmes and measures. The programmes like Jan Dhan Yojana, Aadhar, GST, Ujjwala Yojana, Fasal Bima Yojna, full electrification, Swachh Bharat Abhiyan, Start up India, Houses for all, Skill development, Make in India, Namami Gange and health insurance for poor were launched to change the face of the country. Some steps taken by Modi have potential traction for any coming government. 1400 archaic laws have been repealed. Faster growth in infrastructure like rail, road, coal and power and introduction of GST are commendable.

However, it is now clear that immediate delivery of the government is no match to its earlier ambitious promises. Cow vigilantes have spoiled the peaceful atmosphere required for unhindered growth. Abject surrender of the BJP governments before Karni Sena has upset many liberal followers of Modi. Highly enigmatic and unnecessary step of demonetisation has derailed the growth and, consequently, GDP has come down. Rural distress is all too visible. Jobs which were promised to youth are not coming. Bank scams have captured the imagination of the nation and aspirational spirit is on wane. Dark clouds are gathering on horizon for Modi.

Gujarat has shown some chinks in Modi's armour. Rahul Gandhi has been, somewhat, accepted as mature leader and no one now ridicules him the way earlier he was. He has shown aggression against Modi by attacking on all issues and has inspired his party. He is trotting from temple to temple (very unlike Nehru) to dispel the apprehension of the Muslim appeasement. However, urban Hindu middle class still does not fully trust Rahul Gandhi and suspects his untested capabilities. In the past, Rahul Gandhi has not taken any responsibility and has so far nothing to show except his family.

Vast rural and urban poor and illiterate masses of India have become very clever in the thriving democracy. They have great patience and wisdom and don't give knee-jerk reactions, unlike opposition party spokespersons and channel anchors. Their combined wisdom is beyond electoral surveys. Modi still retains his charisma and is the most popular leader but he has to be on guard. On the other side, a resurgent Rahul Gandhi has to grapple with his very fragile party machinery. Moreover, the Congress has to take along with it its energetic allies. Future belongs to those who can touch the hearts of the people. Modi does this well.

24 February, 2018

National Direction

UPA II had become very quivery by 2013, as was evident by falling economic growth and upward inflation. The nation was appalled by the disclosure of several scams starting from CWG scam. The perception of such bizarre loot of nation's natural resources was so far unheard of in India. The Supreme Court had to cancel the spectrum and coal blocks allotments. The UPA government responded by self inflicted paralysis.

Modi fought his way up in BJP. After this, he challenged the UPA II government by arousing aspirations of all classes and regions and easily dislodged the crumbling regime. People expected rapid growth and jobs. There was increase in growth for next two years but hardly any jobs came for youth. Later growth also slowed down and jobs kept on dodging.

Some senseless efforts like banning beef vitiated the atmosphere apart from ruining the rural economy and the leather industry. More devastating was the cultural shock by activities of some self proclaimed Hindu vigilantes. Some crude efforts to remould historical facts and ludicrous attempts to overstretch ancient Indian glory hampered the intellectual insight.

Many serious economists expected fundamental reforms. Reforms came only incrementally. Bankruptcy provisions and some tinkering of labour laws will not go far. GST can be counted as the only one big tax reform, though it came in a complicated manner, which will yield results only after sometime.

The ease of doing business is hardly visible by way of actual foreign investments. All states are signing MOUs in the Investment Summits, but conversion rate is dismal. Our meritorious but extremely inefficient and corrupt bureaucracy is the biggest hindrance for the ease of doing business. Any attempt, even marginally, to bring bureaucracy to international standard is neither in Modi's agenda nor he is capable of doing this. Like the earlier imperial Congress, BJP has also learned to adjust with bureaucracy in the centre and in the states. There is no desire to reform the police and the lower judiciary. BJP is misusing the police and the CBI as before.

To be fair it may be said that democracy by its very nature doesn't allow so many reforms in different fields in a short time. But the way Modi rose in Indian politics, it was natural to expect all of this from him. All is not despair. There are many programmes of this government which have set the right course. Increased speed in infrastructure sector, Swachh Bharat Abhiyan, Jandhan etc will benefit the country. Ujjwala Yojna has brought a revolutionary change in the life style of the poorest of poor rural women. National Health Protection Scheme, if implemented well, may become a game changer in future.

Modi has aroused tremendous admiration as well as hatred among many countrymen, like Indira Gandhi did in her time. Like her, Modi shares overwhelming dominance over Indian politics. They share many things in common as far as their influence is concerned.

Some of the things which I observed above may be music to the ears of the Congress. Any disenchantment of the public with Modi will be a treasure for it. Some changes in a polity come by default and the Congress heavily banks on it. Congress with reduced role and stature, however, with many state satraps may still challenge Modi successfully. But I don't expect any remarkable change under its present leadership. Congress has lost its vigour and vitality since it has become a dynastic party and its second rank leaders lack the strength to air their views even in private.

All these observations may look to be cynical but there are many sparks which give us sanguine hope for some new direction in future.

8 March, 2018

Strange Marriages

Every Indian political party has shown remarkable flexibility in forging opportunistic alliances. By now almost all parties have worked with each other. Most glaring example of alliance is of BSP and SP, who were sworn enemies. Only notable exception in the foreseeable future is the unlikely alliance of Congress and BJP because both claim to be national parties and are different poles of political fault line. With all sense of responsibility, I may predict that a time may come when even these two parties may come together. This may happen when regional parties will become all powerful and they will discard both BJP and Congress. There is a saying that there are no permanent friends and enemies in politics but only permanent interests.

Since it is beyond the capacity of any party or coalition to solve deep rooted serious problems of India, we the ordinary citizens, can only keep us happy by watching the drama of changing governments.

19 March, 2018

Challenges in Kashmir

No incident of set-back to Armed Forces in recent past has shaken the hearts of Indians as much as the suicide bombing of CRPF convoy in Pulwama killing 40 personnel. For me the loss was more personal as I was Special DG of this very CRPF in Jammu and Kashmir. I expressed my anguish immediately after the incident in my Twitter as under:-

> 'As ex-Spl DG CRPF Jammu #Kashmir, I salute to my martyred soldiers. This is a moment of deep reflection for security and political establishments and not to lose balance of mind. Action should come at right time against real culprits.'

India has been bleeding in J&K for the last three decades. Time has come for us to think and do something pointedly effective, which compels Pakistan to mend its ways and behave as a responsible country and refrain from exporting terrorism. However, this should not be done in a flimsy bravado only to pacify our anger. We should not forget that Pakistan is an irrational nation armed with full nuclear capability. Our response has to be more subtle and some consensus among political parties, civil groups and public at large is the minimum requirement for this.

I hope and wish that India rises to the occasion this time.

25 February, 2019

Allahabad or Prayagraj

Allahabad has been given a new official name Prayagraj. Like all issues of public concern this change has its own supporters and opponents. This holy city is situated on the confluence of Ganga, Yamuna and mythical Saraswati. The city has uninterrupted tradition of pilgrimage since the earliest antiquity. In his time Nehru was moved by Ganga and said that it reminded him of the great heritage of India. Allahabad is also an important city of UP and it is a centre of trade, education, culture and also the seat of High Court, PSC, High and Intermediate School Board, AG office and PHQ etc.

I have been a student of Allahabad University before shifting to Lucknow University. At that time I found that Prayag was a popular second name of the city. Near the University was Prayag Railway Station where we used to go in group for tea at very late hours in the night. There are many institutions with the name of Prayag like famous Prayag Sangeet Samiti. Even sometimes students used to refer to University as Prayag Vishwavidyalaya, even though officially it was Allahabad University. Nearby the university was Bhardwaj Ashram which has been described in great detail by Tulsidas in his famous epic Ramcharit Manas. He has also described the importance of Tirthraj Prayag.

One doesn't require much intelligence to know the motives of the BJP Govt to change the name of this beautiful city. It is purely for electoral calculation and it is also driven by their Hindutva ideology. BJP thinks that this change will polarise people to its benefit. However, the change of the name of Allahabad is not like changing the name of Mughalsarai. There was a long standing demand - Madan Mohan Malviya also wanted this change - for historical and mythological reasons for it. The name of a very ancient city of Turkey, Constantinople had been changed to Istanbul. In this light this change is not a surprise for me but my nostalgia dictates that names like Allahabad High Court and Allahabad University etc. may be retained.

17 October, 2018

General Election 2019

Every general election in independent India had been crucial for various reasons. 2019 general election was also very exciting for more than one reason. Apart from its political ramifications, this election also touched the nadir in public discourse. In a highly polarised political scenario, the worst abuses were hurled by all and sundry. Ardent and blind devotees and bitter haters of Modi were drawn into a war of attrition. Political analysts were also perplexed in predicting the outcome of this election. Almost nobody was prepared to give BJP a full majority and, at the most, saw a new BJP government with the help of many new allies and probably without Modi at the helm. Nobody could even imagine the magnitude of the defeat of the opposition parties everywhere, except in the down south. The miraculous sweep of BJP in UP and in the states, where Congress had defeated BJP barely a few months back, could not be comprehended. Nearly nobody perceived any trend and far less any wave.

I am no admirer of BJP and as a matter of fact I detest some of its extreme ideas about body politic. However, after the dust has settled down after the election results it is time in hindsight to recall the factors responsible for the resounding victory of the BJP. It is noteworthy that the aspirations which were aroused by Modi in 2014 were hardly realised in the last five years. What I feel as the foremost reason for its success is the impact and charisma of Narendra Modi. As a communicator par excellence, he captured the attention of the Indian masses. The people at large believed in his sincerity and integrity and his determination to take the country forward. People believe that Modi is there for 24 × 7 only for the country. He came to be seen as a strong leader. The entire election was for or against Modi. This enthused BJP cadres unlike those of many lukewarm followers of opposition parties.

BJP was also fortunate to have Amit Shah as a relentless organiser of its electoral machinery. He worked with remarkable zeal after his first success in UP in 2014. He kept the BJP election machinery well oiled and kept on strengthening it from one state election to another. One should remember that once he himself worked as booth manager. His planning was always booth centric and he inspired his workers at that level in every constituency.

Indian media, by and large, had been sympathetic to the BJP. The support of the media increased year by year and culminated in a very high pitch before the election. This has certainly worked as a force multiplier for the BJP.

In spite of the gradual economic slowdown (in last quarter of last FY GDP has come down even below 6%), the Modi government successfully launched many schemes which made an impact at the ground level. Ujjwala Yojana, housing for poor, rural electrification, massive construction of infrastructure, opening of crores of Jan Dhan accounts, Swatch Bharat Abhiyan and direct cash benefit for the poor have impacted large sections of Indians in a manner which was not comprehended by the elite political pundits. The implementation of these schemes brought the votes to the BJP in no small measure.

The opposition parties and especially the Congress failed to come out with an effective strategy for the election. Unlike the BJP, the Congress was very slow and clumsy in the formation of the alliances. This hampered the momentum of the opposition's electioneering. The opposition also wasted a lot of time on blaming the EVMs and the Election Commission. The issue of corruption in Rafeal also did not click with the public. The arrival of Priyanka Gandhi on the scene was very late and ill planned. All this made the task of BJP easier. It gave confidence to the party to concentrate on new territories like West Bengal and Odisha.

In the final analysis we have also to accept the earthy common sense of the ordinary Indian voter. It has an innate instinct for deciding the destiny of the nation.

4 June, 2019

Fringe- A New Danger

Sadhvi Pragya belongs to a party and an ideology which stand for Hindutva. There is nothing wrong in being a Hindu or having pride in Hindu religion. But the very basic tenets of Hinduism are tolerance and compassion for everyone. Unlike many other major religions of the world, Hinduism doesn't have one book or just one way of worship. Therefore, it encompasses ideas from all angles. It is surprising and sad that in the name of this religion we had such diehard and narrow minded zealots as Nathuram Godse. He could not tolerate one of the greatest Indians born in its history called Mahatma Gandhi, who followed the true spirit of Hinduism. Godse killed Mahatma out of the hate for nobler ideas. Sadhvi

Pragya has described Godse as a patriot. Coming from Sadhvi this is hardly surprising. She belongs to the same fringe from where Godse derived his inspiration. For sure, presently the mightiest party BJP cannot afford to mainstream such ideas and the party understands this. The vast majority of Hindus are voting for BJP to have a liberal approach into the politics. Another dim witted BJP spokesperson in MP, Saumitra has called Mahatma Gandhi as father of Pakistan. While one has every right to question the political moves and the impact of Mahatma Gandhi in his time, but to call him Father of Pakistan is an insult to the present living population of India.

Obviously BJP is embarrassed by such statements and it has distanced itself from these two statements. Remember, Congress has also distanced itself from certain remarks of Mani Shankar Aiyer. All this is because of the fear of losing votes.

Another dangerous aspect of all such episodes is the role of the electronic media. They pick up only the filth like an electronic microscope and display it ad nauseam. If some stupid persons come out with repulsive statements, it should not be taken as a gold mine for TRP by the media. There are many more other important things before the nation.

17 May, 2019

NRC - An Invited Disaster

In 1980, I was dispatched with a MP Special Armed Force Battalion to Guwahati, Assam to help there in law and order. There was a civil disobedience agitation of monumental dimension, hitherto unknown in independent Indian history. I got the opportunity to see it in several cities and villages. It was an agitation of the Assamese people against the so called Bangladeshi infiltrators.

There had been a constant stream of migration from the then Bengal to Assam from 19th century and this was encouraged by the Assamese landlords for the cheap labour. After partition the migration became on such a large scale that Assamese people felt overwhelmed by Bangladeshis, mostly Muslims. Migrant population put pressure on land and jobs. After the language riots of 1960s, a massive agitation erupted in December 1979. Its demand was to expel all illegal migrants of Bangladesh. This agitation finally ended in Rajiv Gandhi Accord in 1985. It was decided that all the Bangladeshis who entered India after March 1971 will be deported back and this gave rise to the concept of NRC. Supreme Court has upheld the legality of NRC and has insisted for its completion in a time bound manner. The results of this exercise have shocked everyone including the BJP. For BJP it was a shock that a large number of Hindus were declared illegal migrants. The party came out with an idea that Hindu migrants be called refugees while Muslims remain illegal. However, to Assamese even Hindu Bangladeshis are not acceptable. Hemanta Biswa Sarma has declared that it is difficult to accept the NRC for Assam in its present form.

It is surprising that in spite of the experience of NRC in Assam, Amit Shah or say BJP wants to conduct a futile exercise for preparing NRC for the whole of India. Proving one's citizenship by documents is a very difficult task. It will require presenting the documents of one's forefathers and then proving the lineage from them. In a country where documentation is very weak, preparing NRC by this method will be a nightmare for all the countrymen. This will also be a Herculean wastage of administrative efforts. The end results will be erratic and even if illegal migrants are identified, it will be next to impossible to deport them out of India. The question is that if all these practical difficulties are easily foreseen then why the BJP government is insisting on making NRC for whole of India. It is because in theory it looks attractive to ultra nationalists that anybody living illegally in this country should be deported out. But for historical reasons and practical difficulties, this can never be achieved. Definitely there is something else in the mind of BJP. It seems that this exercise will have polarising effect giving the electoral advantage to the party.

The country will pay a very heavy price for this futile exercise. The economy of the country is in shambles and it now looks very clear that BJP is hardly serious about improving the economy. The party wants to win elections only on emotive issues, and it is not putting all its energy on economic front. As earlier I have said many times, the country has very high hopes from Modi because of his strength and courage. The first year of his second tenure is the time to take correct, though unpopular, steps for improving economy. If this time is lost then almost everything is lost and we should forget developing India even as a shadow of China.

22 November, 2019

Chapter - 4

Writings of a Student

O! Man

(I wrote this poem of four rhyming stanzas in 1973, while I was student of Lucknow University)

O ! Man you are walking in dark night,
There vainly looking for a guiding light.
Now in dark, you sing lying on the sea sand,
Confused on this already confused land.

In the purple noon, you have been roaming in
The poppy fields, where you became akin,
With opiate numbness; but gone is now
The lulling balm, you sing with depressed brow.

The sea is kissing the silvery moon,
And there's the ridge tinged with darkness, and soon
The stars will wave in the breeze; but you are
Flooding the vale with gloomy songs bizarre.

Intellect reminds you to go away
From those sad emotions, to have a sway,
Over wild instinct and listless feeling.
O! Man, light will come, if you stop to sing.

18 October, 2020

Changing Values- Past and Present

(This article was published in National Herald, Lucknow on 22 July, 1973. I wrote it when I was student of MA, Previous. It still looks relevant.)

In the dim light of the confused transition of today, one can see the chaotic situation in the camp of established morals. A new, more permissive society is taking shape in our world. Its boundless aspiration is conspicuous in the social arts – in the increasing frankness of today's youth, in blunt often obscene approach in literature, in the candid lyrics of the popular songs, in free fashions and frank advertising. And behind expanding permissiveness in the arts stands a society in transition; a society that has lost its consensus on such crucial issues as sexual honesty, a society that cannot agree on standards of manners on what can be seen and heard. In the changing vicissitudes of the social values, the youth comes across in conflict with the general rhythm and rhyme of the time, creating several problems.

Of concern to the thinking people of the day is the swiftness with which all the old restraints are losing their relevance. Many psychologists and social thinkers see a dangerous swing towards moral collapse and, ultimately, social decay. Extreme conservatives exaggerate the new demands from the youth as the surest way to a horrible turmoil. The greatest problem of the youth is this conventional notion of the grown-ups.

Others, especially the sensitive boys and girls, reject the notion that the new permissiveness is a sign of moral weakness. It is in this context that the more advanced intellectuals come forward with challenging views. Indeed artists and writers hail the new change as a release from the 19th century of repression and hypocrisy. We, the young people, are just beginning to discover the new moral code. Our morality is concerned with how we behave towards each other, and not with how much of our bodies we happen to display.

A crusade is being waged against agencies of moral order–religion, customs etc. Youth is alleged to be turbulent and restless. Nevertheless, the revolution in manners and morals is unlikely to reverse itself. But more inevitability of the change is not sufficient raison d'être for it. Actually, the soul of the conceived change is intellectual freedom, much greater than anything we have known in the past. It is essential to constantly reassess the situation, because the situation will always be changing in such a transitional society.

The above abstract contention is more graphically explained in the western world. In our country, the youth undergoing the same process, has still to fight harder with the problems like bare sustenance. Born in the cradle of want and poverty, our youth hears of the Western luxuries with an air of frustration. The situation, plainly speaking, is not conducive to intellectual progress. Moreover, this provides the temptation to the youth to go towards the left-adventurism. Yet, the economic pressure has not totally shattered the dreams of the youth for a freer society.

The cult of change pervaded our society with the efforts of the people like Raja Ram Mohan Roy. Our renaissance began with thinkers realising the force of Western philosophy. With this realisation, came the sense of inferiority before the West. It was not the usual inferiority complex, we simply found ourselves to be inferior. This sense of inferiority is still prevalent, which is proved by the crude imitation of the West by the pseudosnobs of our present society, who have perverted notions of modernity. India is a country of vast heritage. It has been a land of profound contemplation and unfathomable spiritual power. Definitely our youth is in a condition to donate something to the West. But we have to welcome wholeheartedly all that is relevant in the West. Only a simple acceptance of the situation can end our sense of inferiority. Hypocrisy is noble but simplicity is nobler!

This is the magnitude of the challenge posed before the youth. The aspirations and problems of the youth converge on the same point. Every fresh aspiration generates a score of challenging problems. The attempt to solve these problems itself brings about a change in our environment. Even the most narrow-minded conventional person can never deny change, which has passed into our society. The persons deeply concerned with the morality should better postpone their comments on this change. The attempt of the alarmists to denounce the revolutionary youth is absurd. There is not much advantage in disparaging the moral aspect of any particular change, because the very definition of morality is in flux.

The old taboos are beginning to decay fast. The orthodox circle will die its own poor death. The youth should not bother so much about the old restraints. It should absorb itself in the formation of a new society. Already a new sanguine culture is taking shape out of the ruins of the old order. The new culture and its changed values will be more vivid because there will be fresh air to breathe and no suffocation of morbid morality.

3 October, 2020

Evasion at Nainital

Vice Chancellors Meet

(Published in National Herald on 26 June, 1974 in Letter to Editor Column. I was in MA Final.)

I read with special interest your editorial 'Evasion at Nainital' (National Herald, 23 June, 1974). You have presented a critical, scientific estimation of the conference of Uttar Pradesh vice chancellors. Though no one should doubt the sincerity and ability of our educationists and no one can discredit the conference as a fiasco, yet the proceedings at Nainital will hardly influence the higher educational set-up. It is astonishing that our educationists forgot the major problems. If the omission was deliberate, as it seems to have been, it is even more painful.

You have rightly pointed out the preoccupation of the conference with financial matters. A person having even limited knowledge of university life knows that our set-up can be well regulated within the limits of available funds, in respect of both short and long term requirements. Although emphasis was laid on the proposal for a five-year programme, not even a brief outline of the programme was provided. The conference seems to have worked in a vacuum, in which nothing was known of the much-talked-of Kothari Commission. Even as the vice chancellors were handicapped by the lukewarm attitude of the big guns in the Department of Education, they could have come to the positive conclusions about making education a tool for the social change and for establishing socialism in our country. The first step in this direction could have been taken by working out a job oriented system of education.

It was expected that the conference would also take up the question of attendance. Sometime back, there were unpleasant scenes in Allahabad University on this very issue. Conditions for condoning shortage of attendance should be well defined. Mode of appointments should be proper and only those with merit should get the opportunity.

A score of problems can be reduced if we strictly adhere to a national policy. At present a vice chancellor is so absorbed in his institution that he, however gifted, cannot envisage its place and role in the national set up. We should cease to be nostalgic about past traditions, for the present times need some fundamental changes in our system. Education after all, cannot be divorced from social requirements.

It is pertinent to expect a national conference of educationists, both official and non-official, to evolve principles that can lead to a socially 'good' system of education. Local and zonal approach, howsoever important, are apt to fail. India does not lack intellectuals who can evolve such principles; whether we have the machinery to implement them is a question that may raise some doubt in the present circumstances.

8 October, 2020

Social Service in Syllabus

Should Social Service Be An Important
Part of the Syllabus? WHY?

(My Article Published in National Herald on
16 December, 1973. I was student of
Lucknow University)

Nowadays when the higher education has touched the lowest ebb, both in the fields of academic quality and intellectual pursuit, one should be extremely cautious in airing oracle in this regard. There is a genuine fear that the inclusion of the social service in the curricula may further disintegrate the educational cohesion and gravity. But a closer scrutiny of the problem will show the importance of the social service, beginning from the grassroots level to the apex.

In the present environment, a student generally feels an emotional isolation from the rest of society, and this creates a deep feeling of ennui. This tedium and void of the brain and heart are most conspicuous by the deteriorating interest in studies and sports. Sudden eruption of violence on the part of the students also reflects this psychological state of mind. This feeling of ennui, generated by a number of complex problems, can only be eradicated by giving a student the sense of sharing 'something' with society.

India is desperately steering her course towards development. But a lot of human hours are wasted by the students in the name of long vacations. If the work of the millions of students is modulated so as to be of some use in the rural areas, this will not only give an additional impetus to our stagnant rural world, but it will also lead an individual student to his own moral perfection. Our university population, which has hitherto a perverted notion of modernity, will have an occasion to see the real world, and irrespective of their scholarly achievements, they will be better equipped to deal with the harsh realities in their lives. It is the lack of will, not of logic, that many persons may refuse to see the rationality in the social service.

1 November, 2020

A Picture Post-card

A picture post card sent by me forty years back from Kanyakumari to my friend Ashish on 18-7-1975 reached him at Lucknow on 21-7-1975 - so fast during Emergency. I was on my first visit of south India as an IPS probationer. The letter was found by my friend in his old trash and after its discovery he sent it to me on the Whatsapp.

Text of the letter:-

Kanyakumari

Dearest Ashish, 18-7-1975

I am writing you from the southernmost tip of India. So far I have visited Madras, Mahabalipuram, Pondicherry, Madurai, Rameshwaram, Trivandrum and Cape. Now I will go to Cochin, Bangalore and Mysore. I have visited many sites important from religious, industrial and tourist points of view. I am much excited by this trip. I hope you are well and doing well in your exams.

Yours ever,

24 October, 2016 **N K Tripathi**

Violence in Agitation

(Today, 11 October, is the birth anniversary of Loknayak Jayprakash Narayan. As a student of MA Final, I took part in JP Movement, but I was depressed by its violence. I wrote a short article published in National Herald, Lucknow on 8 April, 1974)

An agitation is essentially a ventilation to air the grievances of a particular section. The student community, which is by far the most conscious part of our society, has been agitating on different issues for a long time. During the British Raj, they shook the foundations of the foreign rule. After India gained freedom, the students have occupied themselves with the issues like the language problem, hostel facilities, attendance and participation in the university administration. What distinguishes the recent agitations of the students in Bihar, Rajasthan and especially in Gujarat, are their wider appeal, because they take up the so called popular clamour as their own cause.

Mass violence which followed these agitations has made the real issues dwindle into the background. The Gujarat agitation was supposed to abolish the corruption in the administration. But what they achieved, or they could achieve in a tangible form, was the dissolution of the popularly elected assembly and that too was achieved with the aid of the black forces that live by corruption themselves. It was not so much the solidarity of the Nav Nirman Samiti that brought the dissolution of the legislature, on the contrary it was the band of goondas hired by the profiteers and a group of misguided labourers who brought the central government to its knees. Hundred people lost their lives in Gujarat.

The administration under Chiman Bhai Patel or Abdul Ghafoor may have been corrupt and inefficient, but the increasing chaos of the students has not only jeopardised the democratic principles but also by creating anarchy it has enhanced the chances of corruption itself. The results attained by such agitations are not genuine and they merely serve the interest of pseudo student leaders. Such student risings should be checkmated by the students themselves.

11 October, 2020

A Teacher

(This poem was written by me in August, 1972 after passing BA to express my gratitude to Mr Raj Bisaria, my teacher of English literature.)

I trod in the darkness of indifference,
As rough sound, I thought poetic eloquence.
Untutored, I lacked any intellect and,
Warm emotions, till I reached your great land.

There I saw on mountains beautiful light,
On seashore, I found melancholic night,

Flowers of different colours – bright and pale,
Romance of life, and saw, sad nightingale.

For last two years, you have been showing us,
Rhythm and rhyme of lyrics fabulous.
However, I blame you for giving
A consciousness which begets sad feeling.

Someone remarked, to think is to be sad,
But I will have this pain, rather being glad.
Now I am a man, full of confidence,
I can trust my own sharp intelligence.

I care not someone else's definitions,
Of life or its various conceptions.
Alas! We will miss your ever dynamic
Entry into the class and your rhetoric.

When old, I will see the University,
I'll recall only your personality.
O Raj! You are a man of life like art.
All that would resonate, what you did impart.

22 November, 2020

A Cruise to The Bahamas

In Peter And Paul Cathedral Petersburg, Russia

A Market on La Rambla, Barcelona, Spain

The Great Pyramid of Giza, Egypt

Chapter - 5

Travel is Life

The Bahamas

I reached this beautiful island of the Bahamas. The cruise brought us from Baltimore (USA) via Orlando to Nassau, the capital of the Bahamas.

The Bahamas, consisting of nearly 700 islands and islets, is a country situated within Lucayan Archipelago in the West Indies. It is located north of Cuba and east of Florida Keys in Atlantic Ocean. Columbus was the first European to see these islands. The Bahamas became a British colony which ultimately got its administrative independence in 1973 under the British crown. It is a very rich country.

Nassau is a very popular cruiseship stop. Apart from the beautiful beaches this town has many pastel-coloured British colonial buildings including the Government House. On a central higher ground of the island, Fort Fincastle is situated from where one can get a panoramic view of the serene beauty. The Bahamas will long linger in my memory.

11 May, 2013

From China

My long held desire since childhood to see Great Wall of China, one of the seven wonders, was fulfilled during my visit to China. This is a massive wall with its total length of 6000 km.This was built by several emperors of different dynesties to protect China from Northern Barbarians.

I visited alone Guangzhau, Beijing and Shanghai in mainland and autonomous cities of China, Hongkong and Macau.

India and China are both very old and glorious civilisations. Both were exploited by the European powers and consequently they became poor.

Both became republic nearly at the same time. China defeated India in 1962 war when it was poorer than India. 40 years back we were equal, but today Chinese economy is five times of us. China has less agricultural land but produces three times of India.

Facebook, twitter and youtube are prohibited in China to keep its people away from international thinking. There are no political rights for Chinese people- no demonstrations, no free media and no opposition and no elections. In India our large poor masses have at least democracy.

I was surprised to see that the vast majority of China does not follow any religion. There are no prayers or rituals, while in India our biggest issue is Ram Janam Bhoomi.

Chinese roads and infrastructure are top class and in some places better than those of US. Their railway stations are very clean and look like airports. Bullet trains are very convenient and common. I travelled in it from Beijing to Shanghai in 5 hours with a speed of 300 km.

We are proud of Indian democracy, but does it mean that we should not do anything as efficiently as Chinese do?

15 July, 2015

Plassey- A Landmark

My interest in the past brought me and Laxmi today to this rather unfrequented place. It was here that Robert Clive of England defeated Siraj ud Daula, Nawab of Greater Bengal.

The battle took place at Palashi (as pronounced locally), Bengal on the river banks of the Hooghly, a distributary of the Ganges. The fighting took place about 150 kilometres north of Calcutta near Murshidabad which was the capital of Bengal at that time. Plassey is the British accent of Palashi.

This very small battle (23 June, 1757), not very fiercely fought, is of huge historic significance as it established Britain over India or say West over East.

As a student of history this place gave me a special thrill!

15 February, 2015

From Russia

It was a great experience to visit Russia which is a transcontinental country. I reached Saint Petersburg from Moscow. Here, I saw Saint Peter and Paul Cathedral and felt it to be the most decorated and glitzy church I have seen, after Saint Peter's Basilica, Vatican. Tzar (emperor) Peter the Great of Russia made it in honour of saints Peter and Paul. Peter the Great founded the city of St Petersburg to commemorate Saint Peter. Saint Petersburg is a port city and a cultural center of Russia. Among other beautiful places Winter Palace is of great grandeur. It was a thrilling visit.

Russia is the largest country in the world with 11 time zones. It stretches from Baltic Sea to Pacific Ocean and from Arctic Sea to Black Sea. Slavs of East Europe consolidated settlements in this area and adopted Orthodox Christianity. Though economically not a big superpower yet it has the second most powerful military in the world. This vast country also has amazing cultural diversity.

I was impressed by the largest and the capital city Moscow situated on the River Moskva. I took a river cruise ride, looking at the grand buildings along the banks. This city looks different from the cities of the West Europe as it has an oriental touch. Kremlin and Red Square are of great historical importance. Saint Basil's Cathedral with its colourful onion shaped domes is a big landmark. I was surprised by the intricate beauty of the Metro stations. I travelled from Moscow to St Petersburg by fast train (200 km/hr) looking into the vast expanse of this country.

Russia is a famous tourist destination, thanks to its rich culture and heritage.

16 September, 2015

New Zealand

New Zealand is one of the most picturesque and fascinating countries I have visited. It is a country of only 48 lakh people but it has made its proud place in the comity of nations. Its people are richer than Americans and live in very healthy and beautiful environment.

New Zealand is situated in the south western Pacific Ocean. It comprises of two big islands called North and South Island. There are about 600 small islands. The total area of New Zealand is 2,68,000 km^2. In South Island there are steep mountains called Southern Alps. Due to its distant location and long isolation New Zealand has bewildering biodiversity. Because of the lack of bigger animals it has many flightless birds and endemic flightless Kiwi is national icon.

After New Zealand was discovered by Europeans, the English people started coming to these islands. In 1840, a treaty was signed between the representatives of the United Kingdom and Marie chief and in 1841 it became a colony of Britain.

New Zealand has highly democratic ethos and its people are very sporting and hospitable. The capital city is Wellington and the most populous city is Auckland. What I can only say as a tourist is that every part of New Zealand is of pristine beauty.

4 May, 2016

Spain- A Happening Place

Once someone is in midst of a happening place like Spain, it becomes difficult to pick some good moments ignoring many other beautiful things. I reached here with Laxmi.

La Rambla is the most famous 1.5 km walking street of beautiful city of Barcelona. This street is the hub of evening and night life with delectable food and wine with thousands of revellers.

Spain with its sun soaked beaches is a popular destination for European and others. Lloret De Mar is the most beautiful beach where men and women just lie under the sun for long time. Marine entertainment is also available. Barcelona has the world class stadium made famous by Massey, a wizard of the game who often comes here to play football.

Barcelona has an opera called Tablao Flamenco Cordobes adjacent to famous La Rambla Street. It is famous for Flamenco dance which is an art form from Andalusia, South Spain. It is accompanied by folkloric music on guitar with hand clapping and finger snapping. The dancer makes beat sound by very fast moving feet with sandals. A visual treat to see!

Like other important capitals of Europe, Madrid is also bewildering in its grandeur. Madrid, Spain's capital is a city of elegant boulevards and expansive, manicured parks such as the Buen Retiro. It is renowned for its rich repositories of European art, including the Prado Museum's works by Goya, Velázquez and other Spanish masters. I enjoyed the experience of Madrid in spite of hot weather.

Spain is like paradise for those who enjoy finer things of life!

18 June, 2017

Great Pyramid of Giza, Egypt

Since school days, when I heard about the Pyramids as the only visible ancient Seven Wonders of the World, I fancied to see them. These pyramids are also the oldest surviving structures built by the human beings.

Egyptian Pharaoh Khufu built this Pyramid of Giza about 4,600 years back as a tomb. It has three chambers including Queen's Chamber and one for Khufu. Khufu's vizier Hemiunu is supposed to be the architect of this colossal structure.

This is built of granite with almost now vanished casing of limestone. This structure is remarkable, apart from its size, for its precision. The base is a square of each side being 230.34 meters (756') and its height is 138.8 meter (originally 146.7 m). It has a very uniform slope of 51 degrees 52" on all four sides. In that period the builders had a great sense of angles and measurements. In all sides of the big base there is no error more than 5.8 cm. The flatness of the huge base is amazing in the limit of ± 15 mms. Stones were cut at the distant quarries and transported by the river Nile.

Precise planning, design and construction without the help of pulleys, wheels and iron tools, the pyramids are real marvel and rightly a wonder. I am fortunate to witness it.

26 September, 2018

Istanbul

Istanbul, historically known as Byzantium and Constantinople, is the most populous city in Turkey and the country's economic, cultural, and historical center. Istanbul is a transcontinental city, straddling the Bosporus strait (which separates Europe and Asia) between the Sea of Marmara and the Black Sea. Its commercial and historical center lies on the European side and about a third of its popu-lation lives on the Asian side. Istanbul is viewed as a bridge between the East and the West.

Istanbul (Constanti-nople) was the seat of Eastern Roman Empire or Byzantine Empire from antiquity to the late middle ages. Later Osman 1 founded the Ottoman Empire and finally captured Constantinople (Istanbul) in 1453 AD. The Ottoman Empire, also historically known as the Turkish Empire or simply Turkey, was a state that controlled much of Southeast Europe, Western Asia and North Africa between the 14th and early 20th centuries.

We took, as every tourist does in Istanbul, a leisurely cruise in the Strait of Bosporus. Dinner and belly dance were on the board. There is a bridge which joins the shores of two outstanding continents. The main sites of attraction for tourists are magnificent Hagia Sophia Museum, Blue Mosque and historical Topkapi Palace.

The Strait of Bosporus is a narrow, natural strait and an internationally significant waterway located in north-western Turkey. It forms the part of the continental boundary between Europe and Asia. The world's narrowest strait, used for international navigation, the Bosporus connects the Black Sea with the Sea of Marmara, and, through Strait of Dardanelles, the Aegean and Mediterranean seas.

Istanbul, a big city of 1.7 m people, is an ideal destination for tourists of varied interests.

30 September, 2018

Chanderi

I visited Chanderi a few days back. I had been here a few times earlier.

Chanderi, known for its fort, is a small town of great importance. It is said that during Mahabharat period it was the capital of the king Shishupal. Chanderi became very coveted in medieval period as it was on way to Malwa, Mewar, ports of Gujarat and Deccan. It was mentioned by distinguished Persian scholar Alberuni in 1030 AD. In its chequered history, it was captured on behalf of Slave Sultan Nasir ud din by his general in 1251 AD. After this it was conquered by Khilji of Malwa, Rana Sanga of Mewar, Babur, Sher Shah Suri and Akbar the Great and Bundela Rajputs. In 1811, it was captured for Daulat Rao Sindhia of Gwalior by a European called Filose.

Presently, Chanderi is a sub division of Ahsoknagar district which is part of Gwalior division of MP. It is famous for its unique and beautiful Chanderi saree.

28 October, 2018

Acropolis of Athens, Greece

We arrived in Athens, Greece just after a hurricane, a most unusual phenomenon for Mediterranean.

We visited Acropolis of Athens, which is on a small hill of immense archaeological importance. Though some remains of thirteenth century BC are present, the most imposing remains are of temple of Athena, the Goddess of peace and victory (427 BC) and the temple of Poseidon, brother of Zeus. Both had fought for supremacy of Athens. Goddess Athena won and brought peace with olive leaves.

Greece is considered the cradle of Western civilisation, being the birthplace of democracy, Western philosophy, Western literature, historiography, political science, major scientific and mathematical principles, and Western drama, as well as the Olympic Games. From the eighth century BC, the Greeks were organised into various independent city-states, known as polis, which spanned the entire Mediterranean region and the Black Sea. Philip of Macedon united most of the Greek mainland in the fourth century BC, with his son Alexander the Great rapidly conquering much of the ancient world, spreading Greek culture and science from the eastern Mediterranean to India. Greece was annexed by Rome in the second century BC, becoming an integral part of the Roman Empire and its successor, the Byzantine Empire and for sometime part of Ottoman Empire. Since 1830 it is a republic.

3 October, 2018

Gaur, West Bengal

I visited with Laxmi the ruined city of Gaur on the border of Bangladesh. A part of these ruins is in Bangladesh. There is mention of Gaur since the times of Chanakya in ancient India, but its location was not certain. For a long time Gaur along with Vanga was synonymous with Bengal.

Most of the former citadel of actual medieval Gaur is located in present-day Malda district of West Bengal, while a smaller part is located in Nawabganj District of Bangladesh. Most of the buildings are the ruins of the beautiful mosques. These were constructed by different Sultans of Bengal before the advent of the Mughals.

This city was on the east bank of the Ganges River, 40 Km (25 mi) downstream from Rajmahal. It was an important river port. However, the current course of the Ganges is far away from the ruins.

The visit astonished me for our varied heritage.

3 January, 2020

Visited Bishnupur

I visited on the first day of the New Year, a wonderful seat of art at Bishnupur in Bankura district of West Bengal. This site is world famous for its unique temples and also for paintings, music, handicrafts and Tussar silk sarees. It was Malla dynasty in 16th and 17th centuries which developed all these arts and built such beautiful terracotta temples which are unsurpassed in whole India. Rasmanch was built by the Malla king Raghunath Singh and it has pyramided shaped roof and a mix of Muslim and Hindu architecture. In Shyamrai (Radha Krishna) temple the minutest possible carvings are made on terracotta walls. In Jor Bagala temple two temples look to be joined together (Jor means joint) and it has very fascinating carvings. There are a few more temples of equal grandeur. It was my one of the most satisfying experiences of visiting temples.

1 January, 2019

Pattaya Beach, Thailand

I and Laxmi reached Pattaya Beach, Thailand. This is one of the most frequented places in South East Asia. This place has beautiful beach with small coral islands and sea sports. Pattaya has developed only in the last fifty years and reflects, unlike India, the determination of Thailand to showcase its tourism.

It is now lined with resort hotels, high-rise condos, shopping malls, cabaret bars and 24-hour clubs. Nearby, hillside Wat Phra Yai Temple features an 18 m tall golden Buddha. The area also features several designer golf courses. Last evening we went for famous ALCAZR dance show, performed by trans women, which is claimed to be second only to the Le Lido of Paris, France.

24 September, 2019

Delegation to America

I led an Indian delegation of officers, four years back, to America on the invitation of US Department of Home Land Security (their Home Ministry). This, I led as DG, National Crime Records Bureau along with my other officers.

The United States Department of Homeland Security is the US federal executive department responsible for public security, comparable to the home ministries of other countries. It came into existence as a response to the September 11, 2001 attack by terrorists on WTC. The then President George W. Bush announced the establishment of the Office of Homeland Security to coordinate "homeland security" efforts by amalgamating large number of departments connected with security. Its stated missions involve anti-terrorism, border security, immigration and customs, cyber security, and disaster prevention and management.

Its one branch maintains the records of all crimes and criminals of United States in a facility situated away from

Washington in picturesque surrounding in West Virginia. We visited this place. Here the data of all criminals and crimes is stored in several servers in the basement of the size of a football ground. We learnt their methods to improve our own Crime and Criminal Tracking and Network Systems (CCTNS). This is an ambitious project of government of India, which I was heading at that time, to link all the police stations and their records in one network so that every criminal or crime can be traced anywhere in India by scientific and computerised analysis. This is a project for creating a comprehensive and integrated system for effective policing through e-Governance.

We visited and met the Deputy Secretary (that means Minister) and other top officials of Department of Homeland Security in Washington DC. We also saw Police Control System in Richmond City, Virginia. We also called on Indian ambassador.

21 January, 2016

Adina Mosque

I visited Adina Mosque today. But for the fact that it is in ruins, the Adina Mosque is the largest mosque in Indian sub-continent. It is situated in the old capital city of Bengal, Pandua. It was commissioned in 1373 AD by the second and an able Sultan Sikandar Shah of the famous Ilyas Shahi dynasty (1342-1487). He had the credit of defeating twice the Sultan of Delhi. This dynasty was established by a brilliant warrior Shamsuddin Ilyas Shah (1342-52). His dazzling victories extended his Sultanate up to Varanasi, Gorakhpur, Kathmandu valley, Kamrup in Assam, Orissa and as far as Arakan coast in Myanmar.

Adina's vast architecture is associated with the hypostyle of the Umayyad Mosque, which was used during the introduction of Islam in new areas. Its construction absorbed materials from pre-Islamic Hindu and Buddhist structures with many intact idols and symbols. The interior of the courtyard is a continuous facade of 92 arches surmounted by a parapet, beyond which the domes of the bays can be seen. The mosque is well maintained by ASI and looks majestic.

11 January, 2020

Brunei

Brunei it was one of the most wondrous exposures in my life in the world. It was a beautiful, clean and glamorous place such that I had never seen. The Jame Asr Hassanil Bolkiah Mosque in Brunei is the ultimate structure I have seen anywhere, including big centres in Islamic world.

I had gone to Brunei as a representative of the Wushu Association of India. I am the President of the MP Wushu Association for last 13 years. Wushu is a remarkable martial art which, like many other martial arts, has originated from China. Wushu's main part is very active and somewhat dangerous fight and it includes action of judo, karate, boxing, taekwondo and wrestling. The other part is safe and artistic display of weapons.

Brunei is a tiny kingdom of only 5765 sq km. divided in two unconnected districts. It is a part of the biggest island of Asia called Borneo. Over two-third of southern Borneo is Indonesia. The upper part is Malaysia and in its midst is tiny Brunei at the northern tip. Its 110 km coast line is on South China Sea. I visited its very dense and beautiful rain forest approachable only by typical long boats. Its population is 4.25 lakh only and its language is Malay. An ASEAN country, its official religion is Sunni Islam and not surprisingly alcohol is prohibited except for foreigners.

The Sultanate of Brunei was established as early as in 13th century (Islam spread that early in a remote island). It came under British rule in eighteenth century and it was freed by them only in 1984. The present sovereign Sultan is 75 years old Hassanil Bolkiah. He is fabulously rich and rules benevolently with gestures like feeding all his subjects on Eid in his palace, Istana Nurul Imam. He has constructed the beautiful mosque I mentioned above.

The Sultan and his family own almost all economic activities in the country. Among many things they own is a marvellous 7-Star Empire Hotel in which even the poorest can visit freely. Brunei has Venice like floating villages in the sea, amusement park, functional polo ground and golf course and many malls. I and Laxmi saw all these places and pictured extensively.

Alas, very few Indians visit this wonderland.

18 August, 2019

In a Street in Auckland, New Zealand

A View From Fort Chanderi, Madhya Pradesh

Carvings on Terracotta, Shyamrai Temple Bishnupur, West Bengal

Grand Hagia Sophia Museum Istanbul, Turkey, Converted into Mosque

Chapter - 6

Economics the Number Game

Demonetisation - A History

A painful period of 50 days is over since commercial banks stopped deposits of old Rs 1000 and 500 notes. The declared objectives of the demonetisation- curbing black money, counterfeit currency and terror funding - will be debated for long and also will be debated its impact on economy.

Millions of people suffered untold misery struggling to retrieve their own money. Millions of daily wagers lost their jobs and small farmers and petty businesses underwent tremendous distress.

A minuscule section of people having black money (also corruption and crime money) became hyperactive and resorted to remarkable ingenuity in converting their money. They also made bankers and many poor account holders corrupt in the process. They were fully successful.

Opposition had been irresponsible in totally obstructing parliament denying the public correct information. A strange thing happened when Govt (treasury benches) also blocked speech of Rahul Gandhi. Modi stood steadfast and kept on changing rules of the game without bothering about media. Opposition was baffled by the public for not creating any unrest.

What will be the benefits of whole exercise? We have hundreds of self-proclaimed economists and experts giving their opinions on this issue. We will see all types of reactions. One thing which is most remarkable is the mature and peaceful response of the people of India in the belief that dishonest may be brought to books. I quote from Forbes magazine:-

> "India is a country that has over 1 billion people, and such a drastic event as the government suddenly telling people that their money no longer has any value could have sent the place into mass hysteria. Although there have been incidents of protest, demonstrations, and occasional bouts of panic, relatively speaking the bulk of Indians seem to have taken to this transition remarkably dutifully. Millions of people have stood in long lines peacefully, enduring rather irritating bureaucratic process that has disrupted their lives, because many believe that it could be better for the country in the end."

30 December, 2016

Pay Commission

The Central Government has accepted the recommendations of the Seventh Pay Commission for pay and pensions. Allowances are still under scrutiny. I would like to react:-

1. The minimum basic salary of Rs 7000 (actually with allowances Rs 15750) has been hiked to Rs 18,000 pm. We must remember that per capita income of Indians was about Rs 7,000 pm in 2014 and this includes Ambanis and Tatas. Minimum wages in MP for unskilled worker is Rs 6,500 pm and for highly skilled worker it is Rs 9,735 pm. The lowest entry level person in the Central Government is totally unskilled but will get Rs 18,000 pm.

2. Highest paid 5 persons getting Rs 1,97,100 will now get Rs 2,50,000 pm. Secretary GOI and DGP level officers are presently getting Rs 1,75,200 will now get Rs 2,25,000 pm.
3. Compared to private sector the Government employees of class IV and III get much more salary doing comperatively less work. Higher level officers get much less than their counterparts in private sector.

   Corruption is rampant in Government at all level and a section of officers has far more money than a hard working private CEO. Some of them are as rich as an industrialist. Actually avenues for corruption and security of job are the incentives for Government jobs at all levels.
4. Looking to our GDP and compared to other countries of the world, we are a country on a higher side for payment to Government machinery.
5. If we compare the efficiency of our bureaucracy with other leading countries, our red tape is notorious. This has frustrated the implementation of policies. Every Government claims to cut red tape but has failed miserably. Even Modi is no hope in this regard.
6. Government officials have huge authority and responsibility but almost no accountability.
7. About one-third employees are defence personnel. They work under very difficult conditions with risk to life but officers of the armed forces are always kept inferior to the civilians. Probably they don't deal with files which may benefit politicians.
8. And yet opposition is not satisfied with the hikes. They want more squeezing of the poor nation to pay pampered machinery.

1 July, 2016

Future Giants

I just completed a book, *'Super Economies America, India, China & the Future of the World'* authored by Raghav Bahal. The book gives great insight into economy, politics and history of these three nations. Tracing their economic and political history, the author ventures to see their potential in 2050. Of course China would be first, America second and India a distant third super economy of the world in that year.

India can do even better but for its rotten and irresponsible leaders. Many important bills of economic reforms are pending in parliament but all the political parties are holding the nation to ransom only to settle their petty selfish scores. India is wasting precious time instead of showing high sense of urgency.

I love democracy but I cannot stand the way our parliament is functioning. It is not known to many in India that British parliament (which we copied) has never been adjourned for a single day in its long history. Some fundamental changes in our system are required. The is for every alert citizen to ponder and act.

4 August, 2015

Steam of Modi

There is something very disturbing about the present situation of our economy. In spite of much advertised measures taken by the government, the economy is sliding. It is feared by many that this trend may not be stopped in near future.

Our demographic advantage has not been tapped. For improving India, we have to move many people from villages to the cities. This means to shift a large section of our population away from agriculture to industry (manufacturing). This will help both sectors. But manufacturing in India is very expensive and our low quality and high priced commodities are not liked by the domestic buyers compared to the better available imported goods. We are also not able to export our non-competitive goods. This is our biggest problem and it is here that we are far behind China. If we have to progress we have to use our big labour force in manufacturing.

Why is our manufacturing expensive and therefore not expanding? Reasons are that we have to work in a particular socio-political environment and it is here that Modi starts losing his steam against a well entrenched system. Our industry is not world class and now sadly Modi is resorting to protectionism by restricting quality import by raising custom duties- something very regressive.

Why are our goods expensive in relation to their quality? It is no secret and many experts have pointed out the reasons. I try to list a few important reasons:-

1. Land is very costly in India. Our land acquisition laws make it costly. Our black money has also put pressure on land prices. Any attempt to improve it will be called anti-farmers.
2. Our formal factory labour is costly. Our informal labour is very cheap whereas a regular labour gets much more. No manufacturer wants more permanent labour in his factory. He employs contract labour or spends in unnecessary expensive machinery to avoid labour. However, any change in labour laws will be dubbed as anti-labour.
3. Transportation of goods by railways is expensive in India. The freight charges are very high because it cross

subsidises the low passenger fares. Any drastic rise in passenger fares will be anti aam admi.

4. Electricity tariffs are on higher side for industry because farmers and urban poor are to be provided electricity below the production cost. Same rate for everyone will be called anti-poor.
5. Farmers will not mind paying for expensive electricity and other inputs if the real and just prices for their crops are available. But high price to farmers will be anti-urban middle class which shouts the loudest.
6. Capital is expensive in India because bank interest rates for loan are very high. This is the result of cumulative mismanagement, political interference and corruption in banks. You cannot fight the past.
7. Enforcement of civil contracts in Indian courts is very dilatory and sub-standard. Same is the case with criminal justice system. Politicians are not reforming it because there are more attractive electoral issues for them.

The above factors are sufficient to retard the growth of industry and export. India can't progress by only service and agriculture sectors. It requires focused energy of several years before it starts yielding results in manufacturing sector. Modi's efforts, if any, may take time but democracy wants quick results and therefore we have more gimmicks (freebies) and populist diversions rather than real solutions.

Any government in power will face the same challenges mentioned above. Some of the factors mentioned above are the old legacy of socialist policies of previous decades. It will be clear to any observer that the real problems are not economic but political in nature. We have to see how much steam is left in Modi to swim against the huge policy structure left behind by the old order.

21 February, 2018

MODI 2.0 - The Economic Front

Modi got a clear majority in 2014 Lok Sabha elections after three decades. He promised to usher in 'a new era' in India and 'good days ahead' for India's people. This victory came on his promise to transform the lives of common men. He stirred the aspirations of poor people for a better future. Modi had declared that he will not dole out alms or subsidy to poor people, but will strive to raise their living standards. People rallied behind him. Modi's manifesto was in sharp contrast to the philosophy of the National Advisory Council headed by Sonia Gandhi during UPA time.

The performance of Modi government on economic front during the last five years had been mixed. With the GDP growing at about 7% annually, India was still the fastest growing big economy in the world. But it was hardly up to the full potential of India. The inflation was well under control mostly due to falling prices of commodities in the international market, especially petroleum. Demonetisation was a setback to the informal sector causing immense hardships to lower and lower-middle classes. The shoddy implementation of GST brought turmoil in the retail marketing. Modi government spent heavily on the infrastructure but failed to create many new jobs.

Fearing unpopularity, Modi turned to various schemes of welfare of populist nature and implemented them with efficiency and zeal never seen before in India. Aided by technology his reach was remarkable. 35.5 crore people were brought into banking system by Jan Dhan Yojna which has accumulated one lakh crore rupees. Under PMAY-G scheme 1.3 crore houses were built in the rural areas which were almost five times what UPA had built. Rural roads and highways were extended at a faster speed. Five crore people were given LPG connections under Ujjwala Yojana.

Electricity has been taken to all corners of India. 9.16 crore toilets have been built and 5.5 lakh villages have been declared ODF. Swatch Bharat Mission has made visible imprint on the Indian landscape. An ambitious scheme of health insurance has been announced which has taken a slow start. The cheapest mobile phone and Internet access in the world were spread across the land. Micro-finance loans reached to 130 million rural households. Aadhaar has been made almost universal and it has been very useful to the beneficiaries for Direct Benefit Transfer.

In spite of the impressive data of performance in these schemes, Modi could not do much for economic reforms. Bankruptcy and Insolvency Law has strengthened the banks and the introduction of GST was the biggest tax reform of free India. Other than these few steps nothing much was done for reforms. Modi government almost continued the policy of populism and welfare schemes of the UPA, albeit with better efficiency. Many economists are even suspecting the official data on GDP.

In his second tenure, the initial one year will be very crucial for Modi and more so for the country. Modi has to find jobs for ever increasing number of young people seeking new opportunities. Fight against black money is far from over. Farmers' distress has to be addressed and in my opinion the only way to improve the lot of farmers is to drastically reduce their number by taking many of them out of the farm sector, and providing them with the jobs in the manufacturing and service sectors. Below 6% GDP growth is reported in the last quarter of 2018–19. Company results in the same quarter show shrinking profit margins. The demand from autos to infrastructure is disturbingly going down. Modi has also to cope with the banks' bad debts.

There is a lurking fear that Modi may not gather courage for big radical call for more difficult economic reforms. What distinguishes India from other advanced countries is the presence of archaic land and labour laws. This makes a mockery of the ease of doing business in India. Similarly Modi may not even attempt to revamp and reform the rotten Indian bureaucratic system and painfully slow judicial system. There is also crying need for reforms in the police system. Unless these systemic reforms are done, India will soon revert to a mediocre country pursuing only populism.

If Modi cannot bring about these big ticket reforms, I think that none else can bring them in several decades to come. There are very high expectations from Modi in his second stint which he has started with a thumping mandate.

20 June, 2019

Weak India and Free Trade

Modi has reached Bangkok to attend the annual meeting of Association of Southeast Asian Nations (ASEAN). ASEAN has 10 member countries of this region. India, like China and Japan and three others are not regular members but have been accorded 'advisory status'. Together all these 10+6 countries want to create RCEP or Regional Comprehensive Economic Partnership.

The RCEP is a proposed Free Trade Area (FTA) between the 10 member states of the ASEAN and its six FTA partners - China, India, Japan, South Korea, Australia and New Zealand. RCEP negotiations began as early as in November 2012 (during UPA II time).

The political squabbling over RCEP in India is due to the basic slowdown of the economy and likely disadvantage of the free trade. The fear is that because of the reduced or no tariffs, India will be flooded with many goods from ASEAN countries, especially China, which are cheaper and this will reduce the demands of domestic goods. In a nutshell, this calls for protectionism where the government protects the local industry by enhancing the custom duties, or as it is called, raising the tariffs barrier. If India signs the RCEP, it has to lower its tariffs. However, I think, in the long run, there are certain advantages to India in its export with creation of Free Trade Area.

Congress has been quick to criticise Modi for likely signing of RCEP. Congress warns that with lower tariffs local industry will suffer. This is ironical because the Congress during UPA II moved in this direction and an agreement was signed with the ASEAN for trade. Now the Congress, through Jairam Ramesh, is objecting to Modi to follow that course. He justifies UPA II saying that the context at that time was different. In other words when Congress does something that is correct, if Modi does the same thing, it is wrong. The intricacies of the trade agreements are beyond the comprehension of an average citizen. Therefore, in the absence of a popular pressure it will be apocalyptic for the Indian economic growth if political consensus is not evolved on the basic rules of economy.

2 November, 2019

Foundation Day of MP

Madhya Pradesh is celebrating its foundation day today. MP has completed 63 years of its existence. On 1st November, 1956 a new State of MP came into being by merger of Madhya Bharat, Vindhya Pradesh, Bhopal State and part of Central Province. This created geographically the largest state of India. It was said at that time that after the reorganisation of the states, whatever was left in the centre of India became Madhya Pradesh. With great difficulty the administrative uniformity was brought into the governance. On 1st November, 2000 the eastern part of the state called Chhattisgarh was fortunately separated and a more coherent administrative unit of MP was left behind.

MP has shown some remarkable achievements in the agriculture sector. It has also registered industrial growth in certain clusters. In spite of all these efforts let us be very clear in our mind that MP is relatively a backward state and requires Herculean efforts to bring it to the average of national development. Human Development Index (HDI) has been created to get a total picture of the state of development of any area. The concept of HDI was evolved surprisingly by a Pakistani economist Mahbub ul Haq with the help of some others. Before commenting further, let us understand the concept of HDI: HDI is a composite index of life expectancy, education, and per capita income indicators, which is used to rank countries or states for human development. In simple words it means the higher HDI indicates more life expectancy, better education and economically more prosperous people.

In 2017, the state of Madhya Pradesh was placed at 33rd rank in HDI among 36 states and UTs of India. The other three states below MP were Jharkhand, Uttar Pradesh and Bihar in that order. This gives the picture of backwardness of MP and other Hindi speaking states in the national context. It is for the leaders and people of Madhya Pradesh to ponder over the future course of action and act accordingly, irrespective of political, social and other differences.

1 November, 2019

Economy Sliding Amidst Strident Politics

Almost all economic parameters in our country are sliding downwards. Many people in India were shocked when the GDP growth of the first quarter of this fiscal year was declared to be 5%. Somehow we wished that this was the lowest point in the cusp of growth. A bigger jolt came in the second quarter when the GDP growth came down to 4.5%. Standard and Poor's downgraded India's debt rating. NSO released its data for September which was very gloomy for manufacturing sector. Industrial output contracted to 4.3%. It was also the worst fall in eight years for Industrial Index of Production. 17 out of 23 industry groups have seen a decline. The core sectors comprising of coal, crude oil, natural gas, refinery products, fertilisers, steel, cement and electricity saw a sharper decline of 5.2%. Of late, inflation is raising its ugly head.

It is not that the government is not responding. It has taken several measures like reducing corporate tax and plan to disinvest PSUs, but these are all very small steps taken very late. Finance Minister Seetharaman had presented a very conservative and non-imaginative budget in February. She had to hastily retract her several steps of absurd provisions like super rich income tax and criminalisation of default in CSR. However, the government still believes that the present economic mess is due to global cyclical pressures. It failed or chose not to see any fundamental fault in our economic policies.

No country can progress without a robust export which boosts its manufacturing and provides jobs and growth. We should forget about the Chinese story which is now far beyond India to even think of emulating. Better, we should now learn from our eastern neighbours like Bangladesh and Vietnam. Indian government and Indian industry are highly jittery of facing the challenges of the competition of world trade. Our goods are of low quality and expensive. This is because of the compulsions of our political class. Our manufacturing is very expensive because of high prices of land, organised labour, electricity and railway freight. These things are expensive due to inefficiency, corruption and political populist expediency. This explains why India was scared of joining RCEP for free trade which requires abolition or lowering of tariffs. India's refusal to join RCEP in ASEAN was applauded by our industry captains and the government is obliging them by resorting to old policy of protectionism.

On conceptual level, there are two divergent views of current situation. On one hand Raghuram Rajan has warned that India is heading towards a gloomy economic depression. Ruchir Sharma, on the other hand, is rather happy to note that the present measures taken by the government will bring the economy on an even keel. However, Ruchir adds that India should forget about achieving GDP growth of 7% or above and should be content with 5% or so. He says his inference is based on the current study of all the major economies of the world. I think India should strive hard to bring wild spirit into the economy by bold second generation reforms. The bold steps required for such reforms are well known and, there is literally an anthology on this issue. If implemented this will make our industry competitive in the world, and its cascading impact will transform our total economy.

An interesting thing is that when economy is sliding, the many of Indians are beholden to the abolition of Article 370 in J&K, verdict of Supreme Court in Ram Janmabhoomi case, abolition of triple talaq and lately Citizenship Amendment Bill. These are the issues where the opinions are highly polarised and a strident discourse is diverting the focus from the economy. The leadership of India is required to focus on economic agenda. The economy of India is throwing a challenge on its face.

17 December, 2019

India's Last Chance for Long Jump

At a time when Modi's political capital is still intact, India faces an exceptionally grim economic situation. An already sharply sliding economy has been bludgeoned by lockdowns in Covid-19 crisis. Moody's downgrading the rating of India after 22 years is a pointer to it. The GDP growth has continuously declined from a high of 8.3% in fiscal 2016–17 to 4.2% in last fiscal. The economy is poised to shrink negatively in the current year. Moody's downgrading shows its lack of confidence in India's capacity to reform its system.

Modi has reassured the nation that India will progress and become self-reliant. He qualified his concept of self-reliance by saying that it means that India should become strong in the global value chain.

India's finance minister Nirmala Sitharaman announced a package of 20.97 lakh crore to revive the economy. She announced various measures in five different tranches. For immediate relief, food grain is being provided to the needy and first instalment of Rs 2000 has been distributed to 9.5 crore farmers. A scheme for providing cheap housing to migrant labourers will be launched. The package provides for a wide variety of credits, including 3 lakh crore to MSME without guarantee. Two lakh crore will be given as credit to 2.5 crore farmers. One lakh crore will be spent for farm-gate by creating agricultural infrastructure. Help will be given to fishermen, animal husbandry and food units. Some cuts in EPF, TDS and TCS have been offered to leave more liquidity with the employers. Rs 40,000 crores will be given as additional grant for MNREGA. Borrowing limit of states has been increased from 3% to 5% on condition of certain reforms by them. The package is short in fiscal and big in monetary reliefs and it is clear that this package is mostly for providing liquidity through banks rather than direct funding by the government budget. Congress and other critics have attacked the government for not giving ten thousand directly in the account of the poor to boost the demand. Government is keen to limit the budget deficit. In any case, we have to see immediate implementation of the package and that is not visible so far.

More important are the announcements of the government's intent for a slew of reforms. P V Narasimha Rao and Manmohan Singh brought the first generation reforms, at a time when Indian economy became totally hopeless. The present situation also leaves Modi with no option but to go all out for reforms. In a crisis, one has the liberty to take tough decisions. The most important, but not clearly described, are the reforms of land, labour, liquidity and legal system. Government has announced to amend Essential Commodities Act and APMC Act to provide open market for agricultural produce. This will give farmers better prices for their produce. The government is determined to privatise all sectors including coal, mining and defence production. A long-awaited step for corporatisation of inefficient ordnance factories is also announced. FDI in defence production has been enhanced from 49% to 74%. Private participation has been opened in space and nuclear fields. The government, if it means business, should come out with details of legislations for these reforms immediately to assure investors. Failing this, no industry will shift from China to India.

The goal of self-reliance should not become a pretext to provide over protection to indigenous industry, otherwise they will start producing costlier goods of inferior quality. The industry should be made competitive and capable of doing export. Indian export is languishing for decades because of costly land, capital, transportation and electricity; and all these are costly because of bad politics and these can be rectified politically. The cost of these inputs has to be reasonable, if India wants to become a strong part in global value chain.

I am not very sure how much determined or capable Modi government is to bring all these reforms in letter and spirit. I had been expecting all these reforms ever since Modi came to power. It will require deft political statesmanship to achieve these objectives. The opposition is certain to create hurdles as it did through Rajya Sabha in 2014–15. Another big hurdle for India's development is its bureaucracy. If Modi fails to eliminate bureaucratic sclerosis, the implementation of all good intentions will become impossible. India has great expectations from Modi and he has the courage and capacity to bring about this change. Such a strong political capital will not be easy to get in a leader in coming decades; it is the last chance for India to unshackle its potential. Modi has to make a concerted and rapid effort to bring a great economic transformation, as China did a few decades back.

7 June, 2020

Slump in GDP

State of economy is something in which not many are interested, and certainly not the politicians. A very cursory attention to the economic affairs is given by media, including social media, ruling and opposition political parties. However, the present slump of 23.9% in the first quarter of this fiscal year (2020-21) is shocking. But this is not surprising and a big collapse of economy was expected. World's fifth and Asia's third largest Economy has fallen the most, more than the next U.K.'s 20.4%. Even before this quarter the economy was growing poorly at 3.1%. Manufacturing has shrunk for three and construction sector for two consecutive quarters before this pandemic era. Covid-19 has totally disrupted an already weak economy. Lockdowns compelled the migration of labourers. By near closure of all productive activities, manufacturing, mining, service and construction suffered heavily. Consumption went down significantly and demand caved in. Many jobs, and consequently income, were lost. In the beginning lockdown was absolutely essential to prepare the health services to meet the challenge of Covid-19 pandemic. But later even after the norms were relaxed by the central government, many states, ruled by different parties, imposed all types of needless restrictions which added to the misery. Even today Railways, buses and metros are not plying normally.

Let me remind here, what I wrote earlier, that Nirmala Sitharaman, finance minister had announced a stimulus package of 20.97 lakh crores to overcome the collapse of economy. She announced various measures in five different tranches. It is high time that some more genuine fiscal stimulus is provided to fire the engines of economy.

What is the way forward? The politicians will be interested only in politics. The incompetent Indian bureaucracy will be of no help for any initiative. It is a wake-up call for PM Modi to apply all his energy on improving economy. Apart from providing stimulus, he has to take unpleasant policy decisions for the overdue reforms in land and labour. He should focus on disinvestment. Department of Investment and Public Asset Management (DIPAM), a timid department, is responsible for disinvestment of assets to muster money for development. For the 2020-21 fiscal, the government has set a disinvestment target of Rs 2.10 lakh crore. Of this, Rs 1.20 lakh crore will come from disinvestment of public sector undertakings and another Rs 90,000 crore from stake sales in financial institutions, including life insurance behemoth LIC. Nothing has been done so far.

Any attempt on the part of Modi to take initiative will invite criticism and ridicule of all opposition parties. Opposition will criticise any action or inaction but will never come out with its own suggestions for improving economy. However, Modi should try to build a consensus with the opposition chief ministers who understand economy better than their national party bosses. In any case, he has to take tough decisions for economy and he has the political strength to do that. Modi should arouse the energy of the nation which should come out to uplift the Indian economy.

The big disruption of Covid-19 can be a boon in disguise for better future of our country.

1 September, 2020

Farm Acts - Contract Farming

I am strongly in favour of reforms brought by Modi government's three Acts - The Farmers Produce Trade and Commerce (Promotion and Facilitation) Act, The Farmers (Empowerment and Protection) Agreement on Price Assurance and Farm Service Act and The Essential Commodities (Amendment) Act. I can understand the frustration and doublespeak of the Congress party. After putting this concept in its manifesto, it is now opposing the Acts. Recently, the party blamed Modi of lacking caliber of Manmohan Singh, but the party hardly gives any importance to the latter's ideas of reforms. Probably, its protest of farm acts is the result of its decisive defeats in 2014 and 2019 parliamentary elections.

Here, I want to highlight the second Act which deals with contract farming. Many opposition leaders are skeptical that poor farmers will not be able to negotiate with powerful private firms. Their doubts are misplaced. Contract farming involves agricultural production being carried out on the basis of an agreement between the buyer and farm producers. Sometimes, it involves the buyer specifying the quality required and the price, with the farmer agreeing to deliver at a future date. More commonly, however, contracts outline conditions for the production of farm products and for their delivery to the buyer's premises. The farmer undertakes to supply agreed quantities of a crop or livestock product, based on the quality standards and delivery requirements of the purchaser. In return, the buyer, usually a company, agrees to buy the product, often at a price that is established in advance. The company also agrees to support the farmer through, e.g., supplying inputs, assisting with land preparation, providing production advice and transporting produce to its premises. Contract farming can be used for many agricultural products, although in developing countries it is less common for staple crops such as rice and maize.

Contract farming has been used for agricultural production for decades in other countries, but its popularity appears to have been increasing in recent years. The use of contracts has become attractive to many farmers because the arrangement can offer both an assured market and access to production support. Contract farming is also of interest to buyers, who seek supplies of products for sale further along the value chain for processing. Processors constitute the main users of contracts, as the guaranteed supply enables them to maximize utilisation of their processing capacity. Contracts with farmers can also reduce risk from disease or weather and facilitate certification, which is being increasingly demanded by advanced markets. There are also potential benefits for national economy as contract farming leads to economy of scale.

However, there are certain pitfalls, which have to be taken care of by the government. The contract between the private firms and the farmers is enforceable but its resolution should be given to some competent agency and not to lower bureaucracy of the districts. Government should encourage farmers' organisations that can negotiate on behalf of the farmers. If the system is made successful for poor farmers in some parts of India, it will convince all the farmers of India about the efficacy of the contract farming and its potential benefits.

1 October, 2020

Chapter - 7

Wisdom from Books

Odyssey

Great Poet Homer

This great epic coming after its prequel Iliad by Homer is a treasure of ancient Greek civilisation. This great poet from Aegean coast has marvellously intertwined the Ancient Greek mythology and legends into folklore. The book is written three thousand years ago as rhapsody or poem of intense force and fluency using six feet in a line. This epic forms the foundation of later Greek culture or we can say of western culture. Its images and metaphors were widely quoted in all subsequent European literature. The best illustration is the romantic English poetry.

The hero of this epic is Odysseus, the king of Ithaca. He left his suckling baby and beautiful wife Penelope to fight war against Troy. The great Trojan War was fought to bring back Helen, wife of Menelaus who was abducted by Paris, king of Troy. War continued for ten years till Troy was destroyed. Odysseus after displaying unusual chivalry could not return home for next ten more years as he was by destiny met with a shipwreck and drifted from island to island. This return journey is the central theme where all manners of gods, goddesses and monsters are depicted in the settings of islands, seas and mountains.

Penelope, the wife of Odysseus, is wooed by 108 nobles who want her to marry one of them, as her husband Odysseus is presumed to be dead. These noble suitors come every day to her house and eat and drink at her expense. At last, Odysseus returned from his epic journey and he along with his now grown up son Telemachus killed all the suitors in his palace. The help rendered by Goddess Athena to Odysseus at all critical junctures is very touching.

Homer has given extensive descriptions of ships and seas. He describes in bewildering details about parts of ships, waves and winds and throws innumerable names of persons and places. His description of clothes, crockery, wines, artifacts, weapons and plants is very elaborate and tells us the advancement of the ancient Hellenic civilisation. Since Hellenic civilisation is the basis of western civilisation, at times I felt as if I am not in ancient time in this epic but somewhere near recent medieval Europe.

So much Greece is the soul of modern western civilisation!

12 February, 2018

History of Man

(Great Curiosity)

The present day man remains curious to know his past. A very short period, hitherto known to man, is called history. Man had been striving to know his evolution and origin. All religions have their version of human past but are not scientifically credible.

I read a book by Jared Diamond, a Pulitzer prize winner, who has brought out a remarkable book with a long title '*Guns Germs & Steel: A History of Everybody for the Last 13,000 Years*'. Apart from the last 13,000 years, even before that, there is a very brief account of 7 million years of human evolution. He has taken a fresh look with new information from various scientific disciplines. Those disciplines include genetics, molecular biology, bio-geography, palaeontology, epidemiology, human diseases, linguistics and, of course, archaeological studies. It also includes histories of technology, writing, political organisation and behavioural ecology. All this knowledge has to be remarkably through one author, who is aided by different experts.

Human history, as something separate from history of animals, began about 7 million years ago in Africa. One population of apes broke away from gorilla and chimpanzee to become our ancestors. After this there was gradual evolution, but we have skeletons of only about one lakh years back which resemble to modern men. They seem to have made some crude stone tools.

In a great landmark by about 13,000 years back, man inhabited all the continents, the last being the American continents. This is also the beginning of village life in a few parts of the world. This was also the end of the last ice age and start of what the geologists term as the Recent Era.

The most revolutionary change in the life of man was when he turned to what is termed as food production, which means domesticating plants and animals and eating the crops and livestock. This all has happened in the last 11,000 years when some part of the human population left the hunter-gatherer lifestyle. Different peoples acquired food production at different times in prehistory. It all started by selecting and growing a few species of plants that were edible and had calories. It was careful selection of different species over thousands of years which developed into agriculture and agrarian society. The food surplus made possible for a large section of people to devote their time for other activities and for many people to become artisan, administrator and commander of military.

The first domestication of plants and animals was done 10,500 years ago in Fertile Crescent, that is South West Asia comprising Iran, Iraq, Syria and adjoining Mediterranean area. They domesticated wheat, peas, olive and in animals sheep and goat. China domesticated 9,500 years ago rice, millet and in animals pig and silk worm. India started agriculture 9,000 years back with sesame and eggplant and domesticated humped cattle. Seeds and animals travelled with men from one part to other and adapted according to the climatic situation. The large land mass of Eurasia is mostly on the same latitude with nearly same amount of daylight and this facilitated travel of crops. It should be borne in the mind that only a few areas of the world developed food production independently. The people of these areas invaded other hunter- gatherers of neighbouring areas who, if they survived, in turn learnt food production. A large number of peoples in remote areas continued to be hunter-gatherers.

Man domesticated only those animals which were available and could be domesticated. Dog was the first to be domesticated in south-west Asia, China and North America. Sheep, goat and pig were domesticated in these areas about 10,000 years back. Cow was domesticated in India 8,000 years back, 6,000 years ago donkey and water buffalo were also domesticated. About 4,500 years back camel and horse were the last to be domesticated. Domestication of horse along with the food reserve created mobile armies moving across the continents.

The livestock was responsible for infecting the human beings by germs. The people living in contact with domestic animals became infected and then immune to germs. Their armies carried these germs and killed vast number of enemy population far more than what their arms could do. Even in recent history, the white people carried their germs to Americas, Australia and New Zealand and their germs killed over 90% of aboriginal population.

With the complexities of society and need for accounting led to the evolution of writing. Sumerians of Mesopotamia were the first to develop writing about 5,000 years back. Writing independently evolved in Egypt (3,000 B.C.), China (1,300 B.C.) and Mexico (600 B.C.). Writing spread in different times to different regions by trade, conquest and religion. Independent inventions of writing and later its adaptations of the invented systems involved socially stratified society with complex and centralised political institutions with necessary food production.

The societies and their organisations underwent many changes by food domestication and increase of population. Initially the hunter-gatherers lived and moved as nomad. Gradually nomads in some areas became bigger and became a tribe of 100 to 500 persons. With food production chiefdom took the place of the tribe and the chief in such society centralised powers in his hand, including the right to distribute some collections. With greater population, the state came into being where the hereditary king was its head having the right to impose tax. With the coming of the kings, the earliest supernatural beliefs developed into established religions. Religion was created by kings to keep their authority. Archaeological evidence shows that all kings started making some structure for worship. Gradually stratified society of the state facilitated the rise of technology. It is to be noted that due to environment and control of food production, we see vast differences in the power and wealth of the societies today.

Jared Diamond takes us to a journey of all the continents in the last thousands of years. He has beautifully synthesised history with biology, ecology and almost all known knowledge.

4 April, 2020

India after Gandhi

- A book by Ramchandra Guha

I just finished an exciting book '*India After Gandhi*' (898 pages) written by eminent historian Ramchandra Guha. This is the history of India from independence to 2008. The writer by naming this period as 'after Gandhi' has given his high regard to Gandhi. I am summarising here the contents as given in the book. The write up below will be a fast- forward for the people of my generation and it will be an interesting recent history for the young people of our country.

The book starts with the partition of the Indian sub-continent. The election of 1946, through separate constituencies for Muslims, led to fierce communal riots and subsequently creation of Pakistan. Congress, Jinnah and the British rulers were all responsible for it in different degrees. Constituent Assembly drafted the Constitution of India after long deliberations. Its most influential makers were Ambedkar, Nehru and Patel. After the partition, refugee influx became the biggest problem for the first PM Nehru. The problem was somehow solved in Punjab but was hopeless in Bengal. Home Minister Patel did a big service to the nation by unifying about 540 princely states by tact or force. Only Kashmir was handled by Nehru with the help of a Kashmiri (secular) leader Sheikh Abdulla.

After the death of Patel, the stage was left free for Nehru. As first PM he abolished Jamindari and reformed Hindu Code bills but did not touch Muslim personal law. He initiated his socialist ideas through Five Year Plan and he became a great architect of planned economic growth through public sector. In foreign matters he adopted the policy of non-alignment which was mostly perceived as anti-American. He was his own foreign minister. He regretted taking Kashmir issue to UN. In 1961, Goa was liberated. Nehru all along misjudged the Chinese intentions on border disputes and gave defence ministry to V K Krishna Menon who proved disastrous. India suffered a crushing and humiliating defeat by China in 1962. Nehru died a forlorn and shattered person.

Nehru was succeeded by pragmatic Lal Bahadur Shastri. He started green revolution in agriculture. His handling of Pakistan war of 1965 was superb, but he unfortunately died shortly after that in Tashkent.

Mrs Indira Gandhi took over as PM in 1966. Congress did not do very well in the states in 1967 elections and a weak Indira split her party and asserted her own authority. She nationalised the banks and coalfields. She abolished Privy Purse of the exprinces. She further tightened the private sector. She did very well in 1971 elections. Her most remarkable achievement was the creation of Bangladesh and decisive defeat of Pakistan. She was now called Goddess Durga.

Shortly after this, things started slipping. Corruption and nepotism were rampant by now and economy remained stagnant. In 1973, it led to JP movement involving students and youths. Indira flouted all traditions by superseding three Supreme Court judges to appoint AN Ray as CJI. She encouraged a committed bureaucracy and made her son Sanjay Gandhi an extra constitutional power. On his advice she imposed Emergency on 26th June, 1975 after her election was declared void by Allahabad High Court judge. Nearly

80,000 political leaders were thrown into jail under MISA. Infamous 42nd Constitution amendment was passed. After 19 months emergency was lifted and Congress suffered a humiliating defeat in North India.

In 1977, Janata Party came to power which was basically a coalition of opposition parties. The next PM, Morarji Desai tried some steps for reforms but clashes of egos of Jagjivan Ram and Charan Singh made a mess and Janata Govt collapsed. Indira Gandhi came back as PM in 1980.

Next more than four years saw no new steps for economy and this was the period when China rapidly started growing. Politically president rule was blatantly misused. Sikh extremism was growing and Bhindranwale (some say he was creation of Congress) became a threat to sovereignty. Ultimately Operation Blue Star of 1984 was launched in Golden Temple. Tanks were used and it is estimated that about 500 troops and 3000 terrorists and pilgrims were killed. A few months later Indira Gandhi was assassinated by her own Sikh gunmen.

Assassination of Indira Gandhi saw the worst rioting which was really a pogrom. Mobs allegedly led by Congress leaders hunted and butchered more than a thousand Sikhs in Delhi and 300 in other cities. Properties of Sikhs were destroyed and looted. Rajiv Gandhi, the next PM, fumbled by commenting 'When a big tree falls, the earth shakes'. No worthwhile police or military action was taken nor were any serious investigations and prosecutions undertaken.

Rajiv Gandhi started with refreshing ideas. He initiated some economic reforms. Unfortunately in Shahbano case he fell into the hands of conservatives and he undid the Supreme Court's decision. This was done only for Muslim votes, but it also had far reaching effects for Congress and the country. He also tried to appease Hindus in Ram temple matter but with no effect. The polarisation of Hindu votes had started. Sending of army to Sri Lanka to fight LTTE proved disastrous. Alleged commission in Bofors case and resignation of Vishwanath Pratap Singh led to the defeat of Congress in 1989 and after that it never got clear majority in Lok Sabha.

V P Singh became PM in 1989 with outside support of BJP. He enforced the recommendations of the Mondal Commission giving reservation to OBCs. His and Chandrasekhar's governments were short lived. Rajiv Gandhi was tragically assassinated in1991. After the elections a minority Congress government under Narasimha Rao came to rule.

The history after this point becomes very recent and therefore the writer does not give chronological account but only certain themes. We have seen that from late sixties country saw the rise of middle castes or OBCs. Political power came into their hands in many parties and new OBC parties later came into existence. This period also saw the rise of regional parties in some states. In nineties casteist parties dominated UP and Bihar. BJP tried to counter caste divisions among Hindus by polarising Hindu votes on Ram Janambhumi temple issue. In this regard Advani's rath yatra was very successful in 1991 for BJP.

Narasimha Rao, helped by his finance minister Manmohan Singh, brought about sweeping and bold changes in economy and led India towards free market. He introduced reforms to liberalise and globalise Indian economy. He, however failed to stop demolition of Babri mosque in 1992 which saw series of riots and Mumbai bomb blasts. After Rao in 1996, short lived third front governments came to rule. In 1998, Atal Bihari Vajpayee became PM. He pushed some more reforms. He failed in his bid to improve relations with Pakistan but valiantly fought and won Kargil war. He launched an ambitious programme to construct the highways. Meanwhile in 1998 Mrs Sonia Gandhi, widow of Rajiv Gandhi became the Congress president. She stopped the disintegration of the party and cobbled an alliance called UPA. It came into power in 2004. Manmohan Singh became the PM while Sonia Gandhi took over as UPA chief.

In this book Ramchandra Guha has given separately a vivid description of the problems of Jammu and Kashmir, North East and Left Wing Extremism.

The author of this book Ramchandra Guha is presently called a liberal intellectual and he is critical of Hindutva politics. I feel that his sense of history is remarkable and he has written this masterpiece dispassionately after diligent research.

20 January, 2018

Uttara Kand of Valmiki Ramayan

A few months back in Delhi in a get-together of IPS officers at ITBP Officers' Mess an intelligent officer gifted me a book UTTARA. This is a translation of Uttara Kand of Valmiki Ramayan by Ms Arshia Sattar who has a PhD from University of Chicago. Valmiki is one of the greatest saint-poets of Sanskrit language. Ms Sattar has translated brilliantly and has successfully brought all the beauty of Sanskrit into English.

Valmiki was the first poet to narrate the story of God Ram. Many scholars including Ms Sattar have concluded that Bal Kand and Uttara Kand in his Ramayan are added centuries later (300 AD). The ideas, tenor, language and very theology of Uttara Kand place it in a different era. Valmiki Ramayan reverberated in whole Indian sub-continent for centuries to come and many versions of its central theme came into different vernacular books. Bhavabhuti wrote a very poignant and emotional play called Uttararamcharit in eighth century. In south, Kamban wrote in Tamil a brilliant book called *Ramavataram*. The latest and perhaps the best was produced by Goswami Tulsidas - *Ramcharitmanas* in Awadhi Hindi.

Ram of Uttara is a king with heavy public duties. He follows the advice given by his Brahmin ministers. He has controlled his human emotions and loves to listen stories of heroic deeds of Ravan in the court told by Agastya muni. Some striking points of this Kand are as under:-

1. When Ram hears from his minister Bhadra about the public gossips of Sita being with Ravan, Ram decides, supported by his ministers, to abandon her. She is despatched with Laxman to Trans Ganga forest near Valmiki ashram. Ram is disturbed but does not show much emotion for Sita.
2. Narad tells Ram that a Shudra cannot perform tapsya. Ram goes out and finds Shambuk, a Shudra performing tapasya. Ram kills him with his own sword. He is hailed by Agastya and others for this work.
3. Ram punishes Laxman, his trusted and beloved brother, for allowing Durvasa Rishi into his chamber. Ram had instructed that he would kill anyone who lets anyone inside his Chamber while he was talking to Kal. Laxman is punished, supported by Brahmins with abandonment. Laxman goes straight away to the banks of the river Saryu and leaves this mortal world.
4. Uttara categorically declares that Ram is an incarnation of God Vishnu. In the last scene Ram along with many other residents goes to river Saryu

and there he enters into the real body of God Vishnu and goes to heaven. All Gods shower flowers on him.

Uttara Kand was written (and added to the original text) at a time when theory of Avtar (incarnations) became well entrenched and central to Hinduism. It is the story of elevation of Ram to divinity and also of reconfiguring of conflict (Ram vs Ravan) as a cosmic one. It depersonalises Rama as a human and his troubles and triumphs, as He is God.

8 August, 2017

The Rise and Fall of Nations

Ruchir Sharma

Nations have an inherent tendency of rising and falling. Economy is the best pointer of a nation and its status is the reflection of social harmony, political vibrancy and an effective and dynamic leadership.

I had been reading for sometime '*The Rise and Fall of Nations*', written by a remarkable person Ruchir Sharma. He is Head of Emerging Markets and Chief Global Strategist at Morgan Stanley Investment Management, New York. He is a top global thinker, who has travelled and studied large number of countries in all the continents. With the help of his team he has scanned vast amount of economic and political data and has come out with very lucid conceptualisation.

Ruchir has gone into great depth of present day political, economic and social conditions of nations. With his analytical study of recent past of the nations he finds out ten clear and interesting rules for identifying the future losers and winners in the global economy. His narration is about how to filter out the hype and noise and pick out the clearest signals that foretell the coming rise and fall of nations. He establishes that a declining population of a nation will slow down its economy. One percent decline in working age people, or say population will result in one percent decline in GDP. Countries with declining population, can flourish only by increasing the age of retirement, adding more women in work force and encouraging immigrants. Even in a big country like China the slow growth of population is now damaging its growth.

Ruchir has given very high emphasis on the political factor in shaping of a nation. He asks "Is the nation ready to back a reformer?" In emerging countries like India the growth can be highly unpredictable and it is here that a fresh leader can make a big difference. It is very obvious that politics matters for economic growth. The fortunes of a nation are better when a new leader rises in wake of a crisis, and on the contrary a nation is likely to be worse off when a stale leader is ruling. There is a circle of life which operates in all countries but at different speed.

The inequality of the distribution of wealth is increasing and while the poor are not getting poorer but the rich are becoming filthy rich. Many leaders try to tax rich heavily and dole out freebies to poor. This populist stance finally collapses the economy forcing the government to go to the 'rightist' policies. The list of billionaires is fast expanding with more bad (unscrupulous) than good billionaires. Bad billionaires own a bloated share of economy and produce their wealth mainly aligning with politicians. A healthy economy requires productive tycoons and not corrupt tycoons.

Apart from above factors, I will briefly mention other pertinent points which Ruchir raises to predict the future of any nation. Is the government meddling more or less? Is the nation making the most of its geographical location? Is investment rising or falling as a share of the economy? Is inflation high or low? Does the country feel its currency cheap or expensive? Is debt growing faster or slower than the economy (GDP)? How is the hype of the global opinion makers watched? Analysing these issues will help assessing the true potential of any economy.

This very readable book is based on research and not on perception. With many yardsticks he sums up by taking the reader to a journey of the world and tells us likely winners or losers in the near future. As far as India is considered his assessment of its economy and geography places it in a rising mode.

4 September, 2018

Thus Spoke Zarathustra

- A Masterpiece

I recently read this better known book of Friedrich Nietzsche, translated from German into English by Kaufmann. Before I say anything, I am quoting some of the lines (epigrams) from the book that I have chosen:-

> "This old saint in the forest has not yet heard anything of this, that God is dead!"
>
> "Once you were apes, and even now, too, man is more ape than any ape."
>
> "I love him who makes his virtue his addiction and his catastrophe: for his virtue's sake he wants to live on and to live no longer."
>
> "I am not the mouth for these ears."
>
> "One no longer becomes poor or rich; both require too much exertion."
>
> "There is ice in their laughter."
>
> "In a friend one should have one's best enemy."

The book is full of such rather enigmatic expressions and for me or probably for any ordinary reader it is not very readable or comprehensible unless seen in a context. The book is as much of philosophy as of literature. In reality it may be called a complex quintessence of European thought till the end of the nineteenth century.

A very brief account of Nietzsche may be relevant here. He was born in 1844 as a son of a clergyman in a small German town and ironically became in such a family a disbeliever to announce 'God is dead'. His father died when he was five and at 24 he was appointed as a professor of philology. By 35 years of age he resigned due to chronic illness and moved around Europe on his meagre pension. Next ten years he wrote in tremendous physical pain of paralysing migraine, stomach cramps, insomnia and extreme myopia. He became insane at the age of 45 and died at 56 (in 1900). His ranges of interest are bewildering— from aesthetics to atheism, existentialism to ontology and from poetry to psychology.

Zarathustra was the old sage of Persia who started Parsee religion. Nietzsche's Zarathustra, though a sage, is completely different and is only for highly allegorical genre. There is no plot as such and it is wandering sage's uttering which is the theme. Nietzsche annihilates the traditional belief in God and Christianity and laughs over traditional morality and virtues. He gives a dazzling concept of overman (superman) which is his goal. According to him present man is between ape and overman. He independently of Freud puts the concept of psychoanalysis in the novel. The philosophy of 'eternal recurrence' is the mainstay of this book which means all the events in one's life will happen again and again infinitely.

There is a new concept in this book which is the 'will to power' and this is the fundamental component of the human identity. Everything we do is an expression of the will to power and the will to power is the force behind man's struggle against his surrounding environment as well as his reason for living in it.

Nietzsche's style, though looks serious in form is actually full of a peculiar sense of humour and this book is also categorised as comedic. There is abundance of the epigrams, the wit and the sarcasm. There is fusion of satire and seriousness, pathos and pun along with a strong philosophical message for the mankind.

This book opens an intellectual door to new understanding of man and his complexities. A reading of this book gives an idea why Nietzsche was rediscovered in the second half of the twentieth century and is still relevant in realm of ideas!

5 June, 2018

Great Journey of Genius of Mathematics

During the period of my recent convalescence for toe fracture, which I got during some exercise, I came across a wonderful book by William Dunham titled '*Journey through Genius-The Great Theorems of Mathematics*'. It is not a book of dull calculations but a fantastic work of art. It has historical perspective with biographical input of some of the giant thinkers of mathematics who made possible the present civilisation. Except for some later chapters, the book requires only school level memories.

About 15000 years back Man left hunting and started agriculture. This necessitated some rudimentary arithmetic for counting exchange of crops and some geometry to compare the sizes of fields. The development of early geometry came first due to the construction activities at the dawn of civilisation. About 4000 years ago Egyptians required constructing a right angle for early pyramids. They took 12 ropes of equal length and tied them into a loop. Then they spread on ground 5 ropes in a straight line and then pulling the joint of 3 and 4 ropes made a triangle of sides 3, 4 and 5. The angle between short sides was a right angle.

The real logical thinking started in Greek world. All sciences and philosophies were born in its cradle. The earliest known mathematician was Thales who in sixth century BC said that no statement can be accepted for its intuitive plausibility, but it has to be subjected to a rigorous logical proof. He proved among other theorems that the sum of angles of a triangle is equal to two right angles. He found that an angle inscribed in a semi-circle is a right angle. Just afterward came a great thinker Pythagoras who gave the well known theorem that sum of the squares of the two sides of a right angle triangle is equal to the square of the hypotenuse. His other striking discovery was of irrational numbers as against whole number. This was not arithmetic but geometry which led to all this. In a right angle triangle if two sides are say 1 each then hypotenuse will be under root of two-something which is not a whole number but is real.

There came a great mathematician around 300 BC called Euclid who was very sharp and he broadened the limits of knowledge. It was he who proved logically Pythagorean Theorem. He found that a cone is one-third of a cylinder of the same base and height. He examined many solid geometrical shapes. He also discovered geometric algebra. He explored numbers and postulated many fundamentals including infinitude of Prime numbers.

Greatest of all Greeks was Archimedes of Sicily of Eureka fame. Density was his very minor concept as he was basically a brilliant mathematician. As a man he was always lost in thinking and it is recorded that he asked for some extra time to solve a problem when Roman soldiers came to kill him. Soldiers did not oblige and he gave away his life. His biggest breakthrough was the formula for area of circle and polygons. He established link between circumference and the circular area. He found surface area of a cylinder and a sphere. His climax is when he summed up, by proudly declaring, that any cylinder circumscribed about a sphere (i.e. exactly fitting) is 'half again' (he means one and a half times) of the sphere both in area and volume!

With the decline of Hellenic civilisation all developments took a nosedive. Only Heron in first century AD did some work like formula of a triangular area. He also found by calculation the circumference of the world which is very close to the reality. In Middle Ages Muslim world became the hub of knowledge but of very limited initiative. In ninth century one Arab called Mohammed ibn Musa al Khowarizmi gave rise to Algebra (word derived from his book) with solutions of linear and quadratic equations. Zero (0) travelled from India to Europe through Muslims. Indian mathematician Bhaskara found value of 'pi' to be 3.1416. Renaissance after 14th century brought mathematics back to Europe beginning with Cardano who gave solution of the cubic.

A great gem, Newton was born in 1642 and lived a long life. He was a unique person and did his all far reaching revolutionary work in mathematics and physics by the time he was only 25. His work included Binomial Theorem. He discovered both differential and integral calculus. He worked on light but more than anything his scientific fame rests on his perfectly embryonic theory of universal gravitation. He never entered into any competition with other persons but once when he was challenged by Bernoulli he reluctantly responded. Bernoulli asked to find out a curve in which a ball will roll down the fastest. No one could solve it in whole Europe including famous Leibniz in the given period of six months. Finally the letter of challenge reached at midnight when a tired Newton reached his house. Newton found the solution in a few hours in one sitting on that late night.

The legacy of Euler is unsurpassed in history of mathematics. In both quantity and quality, his achievements are over-whelming. Born in Switzerland, trained by Johann Bernoulli he mostly worked in St Petersburg, Russia. He had fantastic brain. He could recite things like 241 raised to the power 4 etc. He could do difficult calculations mentally up to 50 places with accuracy. The sum of the series 1+1/4+1/9+1/16+-- was known to be less than 2 but exact value was not found by even Leibniz. Euler found it to be pi square/6 or 1.6449...Euler was successful in evaluating complicated infinite series. Nineteenth century had no single great mathematician but an array of many scholars who pushed the frontiers of the subject. It became much more abstract and looked away from reality. Cantor, a brilliant mathematician, took the challenge of infinite and created a marvellous set theory. He proved that set of all algebraic numbers is denumerable. He went into the realm of transfinite and explored nature of infinite cardinals. Mathematics in twentieth century became not a tool for other sciences but an abstract art for its own sake.

In the end I quote Bertrand Russell: "our entire mathematics, rightly viewed, possesses not only truth, but supreme beauty— a beauty cold and austere... "!

27 July, 2018

Chapter - 8

Men in Uniform

Armed Martyrs

I had a very grim experience as a CRPF officer when I was called to head its headquarters immediately after the massacre of 76 CRPF men in Chintalnar, Chhattisgarh by Naxals on April 6, 2010. At that time I was under tremendous pressure from media, agitated officers of the home ministry (who are accountable for nothing) and above all from hyper quick the then Home Minister, Mr P. Chidambaram. The scenario of the spot was tragic. BJP was shouting at the top of the pitch for the so called mistakes and cowardice of the Congress Government. Media became all knowing and started giving absurd unsolicited advice. The government (MHA) did only what they are expected to do i.e. appointing a committee to look into the incident and suggest remedial measures. Later nothing much happened by way of gadgets, training or tactics or command and control. Soon my and nation's attention was diverted to J & K for unprecedented violence where I happened to be in command of CRPF.

While the present incident of ambush near Burkapal, Sukma is very unfortunate, the reaction is similar. Mainstream media (English) is again very damaging in debating the issue in political acrimony and making irrelevant comments. One senior anchor reminded the boasting of 56 inches chest during the election campaign and demonetisation to score a point. Congress attacked as earlier BJP used to do by hard hitting taunts.

The political and bureaucratic leadership have played havoc in India on internal and external security. Ministry of Defence cannot buy weapons in time and not without the allegations of huge corruption. MHA wants to control the paramilitary forces in total subordination. Uniform officers are hardly given any respect or freedom to work. Till date our armed forces have no centralised commander. Look the way China is reorganising its forces very fast according to the present requirements.

Fortunately, Indian troops are very courageous and disciplined and are fighting on all fronts in spite of many shortcomings. They are prepared to die so that nation can live.

26 April, 2017

Poor Armed Forces

We all are very proud of our Army, Air Force and Navy. They defend our frontiers and bring glory to the nation, while they are always ready for supreme sacrifice - their lives. They are the defenders of the very existence of the nation.

All our leaders, including the prime minister, are not tired of praising armed forces. But sadly this happens only when there is tension on the border or during war. After Uri now there is hysteria to teach a lesson to Pakistan. Who will teach this lesson if not our armed forces? But once the tension is over the armed forces are forgotten or even humiliated.

Not many bother to know that the pay hike suggested by the 7th pay commission has been rejected by the forces due to certain anomalies on core issues. All three Chiefs have issued orders on 9th September to accounts not to implement new pay scales.

An IAS officer posted in north-east may get up to Rs 60000 as special pay. An army officer posted even in Siachin will get half of it. Politicians and bureaucrats in Defence ministry take decades to purchase arms and at times with huge bribes. The services Chiefs are humiliated on files by babus in the government for minor issues.

The people and the government of any great nation are recognised by how well they treat their forces in peace time!

25 September, 2016

FIR on Army

On 27 January, 2018 an Army convoy was stoned by a mob in Shopian in South Kashmir. In the retaliatory firing by the Army convoy, two persons were killed. An FIR was lodged in the local police station. Shopian is the same place where in 2009 a false case was registered against the armed forces for the alleged rape and murder of two girls. Should an FIR be lodged against the armed forces for an act done during the discharge of their duties?

Kashmir is declared a disturbed area under Armed Forces Special Powers Act better known as AFSPA. In a disturbed area it gives some special protection to the Armed Forces and the Central Police Forces. It also confers many powers for maintaining law and order like searches etc. One important power is to open fire:-

> "After giving such due warning, fire upon or use other kinds of force even if it causes death, against the person who is acting against law or order in the disturbed area for the maintenance of public order."

In the present case this power could have been sufficient justification of firing by army. However, in a surprising move Army has to come out with an explanation that it fired in self defence. Such statement was unwarranted.

Regarding this FIR, it has been propagated that this time something extraordinary has happened. In my understanding such FIRs have also been registered earlier. Secondly, it is made out that FIR has been registered against the Major. Actually FIR has been registered against unknown persons of the army convoy led by the named Major. Important thing to notice is that based on this FIR there can be no prosecution in the court of law:-

> "Army officers have legal immunity for their actions. There can be no prosecution, suit or any other legal proceeding against anyone acting under that law."

In view of these provisions, this FIR will be infructuous as had been earlier FIRs. However, one is to be reminded that Central Government has the authority to allow prosecution in such cases if it deems fit and it has used this power in much publicised Machil case of 2010 against the army.

It will be in the interest of the nation that army should speak less and speak only through actions. More dangerous is when myopic and selfish politicians start commenting on technical details.

Kashmir is a very sensitive as well as complicated issue. Right from the time of its merger in India, no solution has been found agreeable to all stakeholders. Even Nehru faulted and later regretted taking this issue to UN. Apart from the last three decades of terrorism, at present Kashmir has become the testing ground of the might of mischief of Pakistan and more so of China.

1 February, 2018

Shame

I joined a discussion on IBC24 TV on a very disturbing gruesome gang rape of a daughter of a police parents reported in Bhopal.

Far more shocking in this incident was the disgusting behaviour of the police officers. The girl and the family of the victim suffered double whammy when they roamed from one police station to another police station begging to register their complaint.

This was in the main area of the capital of MP which was in the festive mood for the Foundation Day ceremonies.

Decades of training for sensitising policemen towards gender issues has gone down the drains. I believe now officers and politicians will take some action in this case, since it has been highlighted in the media. It has become a trend that police only comes into quick action when the media takes up any issue with full facts.

I hang my head in shame as a former policeman.

3 November, 2017

Police Officers Mess

When we entered the IPS, we were told that police mess is our second home. Though one has to follow all the etiquettes and decorum, but more importantly there has to be an emotional attachment with the mess. When I joined MP cadre, I was fascinated by the locational beauty of the Bhopal Police Mess.

Ever since then, I as well as this mess had gone through many changing vicissitudes, mainly in our outer forms, while the basic spirit remains the same. Yesterday while attending a farewell party in the mess, I had a sense of deep satisfaction

while recollecting the years bygone. I hope that in my life there will be many more occasions on this beautiful lakeside mess to look before and after.

2 March, 2019

Chapter - 9

Beyond Our Borders

Doklam Standoff

Exactly two years back I was on the great Chinese wall, fulfilling my childhood ambition.

The attitude of Chinese people and media then was very friendly towards India. Modi was well known to the public and it seemed as if these two giants and ancient civilisations of Asia would march together. Sadly at present we have eye ball to eye ball confrontation in Doklam, a tiny part of a small plateau in Bhutan. Chinese media (and now also Govt) is breathing fire reminding us of humiliating defeat of India in 1962.

In 1962, India was having stronger economy than China. We lost the war because we never thought of it. From 1978 onward when Deng Xiaoping started all round reforms, China very slowly overtook India and then steamrolled ferociously on economic development. China surprised the world by its massive infrastructure and gigantic manufacturing.

Today Chinese economy is five times of India in size and so is its military might. It has only US left to surpass. In this scenario Modi has shown considerable courage and diplomatic maturity in the Doklam standoff. I hope we will neither succumb nor be over jingoistic.

19 July, 2017

Howdy Modi

During an official visit in Washington in 2011, there I got an official opportunity to meet formally the Ambassador of India in the Indian embassy. The Ambassador told us that the diplomacy is a hard work and requires relentless efforts in multi-dimensional spheres. The symbolism of the political leaders, sometimes, may have a mismatch with the reality.

It is now about two weeks when Trump joined Modi in an ultra-glittering mega show at Houston, US. The glaring optics and the rhetoric of this spectacle took the world with surprise and envy. It was music to the Indian ears when Trump declared that we have to confront the menace of Islamic terrorism. No Indian leader can dare utter the words 'Islamic terrorism'. Modi in his resounding speech claimed that everything is fine in India and hoped that the friendship between India and US will flourish. India was especially delighted that strident message from Howdy Modi would frustrate Pakistan, and at the same time iron out commercial fissures in Indo-US trade.

A few days later Trump addressed formally at UNGC and it surprised and disappointed many Indians that he did not utter a single word against terrorism. For the discerning observer, it was clear that there was a sort of overleap on the issue of terrorism in the deliberations at UNGC. This is a scary situation for India to ponder. It may leave India all alone to fight its own war on terror.

During Modi's visit there was also no agreement on trade. Fortunately the talks are still continuing between the officials of the two sides. It is likely that in a few weeks time, some agreement may emerge after India yields considerable ground on custom duties. India may also concede on

Harley Davidson bike which is a personal fancy for the President Trump.

India has to adhere precariously and continuously to its relations with two other global giants, Russia and China. In the last couple of years India had been reaffirming its old traditional friendship with Russia. With China we have far more complicated relationship with strategic advantage being with China. China which is five times bigger in economy and with a far superior military can be held only by showing the carrot of Indian markets. In this context it will be interesting to watch Indian response to Huawei for 5G.

However, in the final analysis it is America which is of paramount strategic importance to India to counterpoise China, and also by default Russia. For US also there is no alternative, in what it calls Indo-Pacific region, to contain Chinese influence except by making a nexus with India and Japan. In this sense we are assured of continued American support for our survival in front of hostile military powers. But America will be unrelenting with India in its commercial interests and immigration policies. America will also leave India alone to fight Pakistani terrorism. Indian diplomacy has to keep pace behind the scene of dazzling lights of Houston.

7 October, 2019

Dragon and Elephant - Delicate Diplomacy

In the Chinese city of Wuhan, Narendra Modi and Xi Jinping held an informal summit. Both sides went into the summit with low expectations. India always finds China very enigmatic and also it had very bitter experiences with its neighbour, latest being the standoff of Doklam and stiff Chinese opposition of India on international forums.

India's concerns are mainly twofold. First is the tension on disputed borders and territories, aggravated by the fact that China has far more military muscles than India. Any easing of tension in the Himalayas would be a big relief for it. The second concern is the balance of the trade. Any major opening for Indian exports into China will boost the Indian manufacturing and service sectors.

Chinese interest lies in Indian support for the globalisation in trade and tacit support for One Belt One Road mega project. China is aware not to push India totally into the lap of America. On the other hand India is finding Russia moving to the side of China and Pakistan. India also feels that America is not supporting it as strongly as India would like it to do. Therefore, there is some possible space for understanding and cooperation between India and China.

Xi Jinping feels very confident of himself after being declared as president for the life. Modi has emerged as an astute diplomat who can dare take risks. All this gives some strength to this informal summit of Wuhan to take strides in positive direction.

29 April, 2018

Trump has fallen– Not Trumpism

Trump has fallen but only after giving a very dogged fight. It was earlier predicted by several polls that Trump will be trounced by the Democrats, but this did not happen. This point should not be lost to visualise the future of America for next four years. Trump has left a bitter legacy of a very hostile polarisation in American society, which will hinder the easy course for the new President-elect Joseph Biden. Trump is gone but the shadows of Trumpism will linger long.

There are genuine ideological differences between Republicans and Democrats. These differences have given different visions to the warring presidential candidates. For Trump the rallying call for his supporters was his drastic curbing of illegal (and legal) immigration. Trump stood for economic deregulation and tax cuts for the rich. He wanted to establish a deeply conservative judiciary and a strong law and order to stoke fear among those who wanted justice for equality. Trump was a queer Republican; away from its mainstream and carving out his own racist following. He channelised the frustration of middle class and lower middle class rural whites, into anger against all enterprising liberals. Apart from this vision, Trump had his natural traits of racism, narcissism, sexism and bigotry. With these traits Trump played havoc with the normal democratic functioning and polarised dangerously the American society, probably for a long time to come.

Joseph Biden has a conciliatory view for the racial conflict and he eschews any racial appeals. He wants to address to the rising economic inequality and promote harmony and social justice. He is more likely to heed to the scientific experts to deal better with the crisis of Covid-19. He is also likely to go back to Paris Agreement for climate change and assume greater responsibility for many international causes. He may pursue the Trump's policy of non-involvement in Afghanistan and West Asia. Biden will be compelled to take a strong stance against China, even though he would like to melt down in trade issues with it. India may not be unduly concerned, but Biden will not turn a complete blind eye to human rights issues in Kashmir and policies of majoritarianism. Modi will not be much at ease with the new incumbent.

Anyone who has a deep insight into the American democratic system would have noticed that the electoral system in the US has a strong bias in favour of rural and small White populated states. A small state of five lakh population Wyoming has 3 electoral college votes, while California with its four crore population, which is 80 times of the Wyoming, has only 18 times of electoral college votes. More blazing is that all states send two representatives to Senate irrespective of their size. It is also noteworthy, that Senate approves many important appointments, including the judges. The whole system favours the people like Trump.

Now for Trump, I hope, he will refrain from fanning racial and social strife. He should also make a clean concession speech. Biden has a very onerous job of uniting the badly fractured and divided America. His agenda is very ambitious but his opportunities are limited. With skewed strength against him in Senate and Supreme Court, he will be frustrated to implement his many programmes. However, his strength lies in the support of all right-thinking Americans and the goodwill of the majority of the international community.

12 November, 2020

Museum Converted into Mosque

— Disturbing Notes From Turkey

World famous landmark of Istanbul, historical Hagia Sophia Museum has been converted into a mosque. Turkish President Recep Tayyip Erdogan has ordered the Hagia Sophia museum, Istanbul's most beautiful building, to be converted into a mosque. He has taken this populist decision to appease the religious feelings to get political benefit at a time when his popularity is sagging. The status of the building, which received 3.7 million visitors last year, has served as a rallying cry for Mr Erdogan's conservative and nationalist base, and the president has used this issue to distract voters.

I and my wife visited this splendid museum in September, 2018. I took this picture of Laxmi in this building. I was awe-struck by its grandeur. It was interesting for us to see that this domed site retains its Christian iconography, and to learn that the minarets were added later, when it became a mosque for the first time.

The Hagia Sophia, a major draw for the tourists, has a long and complicated history. This architectural marvel was built as a church by the Byzantines in the 6th century. Later it was converted to a mosque after the conquest of Constantinople (Istanbul) by Islamic Ottoman Sultan Mehmet II in 1453. In 1934, Turkish leader Mustafa Kemal Ataturk's Cabinet decreed that it be turned into a museum. Ataturk was one of the greatest persons of the 20th century, who abolished the Caliphate and created a Republic of Turkey. He was deeply secular and modern in outlook and abolished all the Islamic laws and replaced them with secular European laws. He abolished polygamy and purdah and gave equal rights to women and minorities. It was in this spirit that he converted this building, claimed by Christians and Muslims, into a museum. Now it is a World Heritage declared by UNESCO. It is widely regarded as a symbol of peaceful religious coexistence.

The present conversion into mosque has been widely condemned by international community. Most vociferous protest has come from the US, Russia and Greece. Many other Western countries have also criticised this step and feared that the minorities in Turkey may not feel safe. UNESCO had also appealed to maintain the status of this building of heritage value.

There had been many anguished comments by distinguished persons. Patriarch Bartholomev, spiritual leader of Orthodox Christians warned that the museum is a place where "East is embraced with the West" — and if converted, it would "fracture these two worlds." U.S. Secretary of State, Mike Pompeo had earlier said converting the Hagia Sophia would limit "its unsurpassed ability — so rare in the modern world — to serve humanity as a much-needed bridge between those of differing faiths, traditions and cultures."

Turkey started very promisingly in the beginning of the 20th century and is now rolling down in the 21st. It was a citadel of liberalism and secularism in whole Islamic world. It will be a big setback to all the liberal and secular leaders and peoples of the world. Having visited this magnificent place, I am personally disheartened.

14 July, 2020

Chapter - 10

Yearning for Governance

Breaking News

This may not look like breaking news to those who are used to a staple diet of trivial but sensational non-issues.

The breaking news is that the Indian Parliament is not functioning for the last five days. With great difficulty one bill on the transgender was passed in Lok Sabha. This was hardly debated and, as usual, is half-baked and flawed. There is complete breakdown and ruckus in both houses on the issue of corruption in the Rafale deal. The government is ready for a debate because it considers itself armed with Supreme Court judgement. Congress and the opposition are relentless because of certain facts and are making this issue as the central theme for 2019 Lok Sabha elections.

Blocking the proceedings of the Parliament and thereby blocking the aspirations of the millions of electorates has become a regular way of life of our democracy since 2011. Before 2011 there were many occasions when Parliament could not function, but what was the new innovation by the then opposition BJP, was the complete washout of session after session of the Parliament. On the demand of the JPC for 2G spectrum case, several sessions of Parliament were sacrificed. After 2G it became a routine for the BJP to block the working of the Parliament and not allow UPA II government to function. This gave a weird argument to the BJP that there is a complete paralysis in the UPA II. This tendency continued till 2014 Lok Sabha elections.

It was not surprising that after 2014 the Congress and the opposition started doing the same what they had learnt and faced from BJP. Since Congress was decimated in the Lok Sabha, it blocked the Rajya Sabha where it was in strength. As a result Rajya Sabha was kept in hibernation. The most significant economic reforms in land and labour sectors were buried in the din of the house.

The idea of blocking the proceedings of the Parliament is very simple. The opposition simply doesn't want the government to come out with any measures which may be beneficial to it. Therefore, the opposition wants that the Parliament should not function on the pretext of some big issue like 2G, CWG, Coal Scam or now Rafale.

The mother of our Parliament is the British parliament. The British parliament is presently undergoing the bitterest phase in its life after the Second World War and the issue there is the Brexit. In spite of the bitterness among the parties and intra party, there is no blocking of the proceedings and every member is heard with full attention. However, we have taken only the forms from the British system, but we have still not risen above from our old feudal and undisciplined instincts where any dissenting note is not worth giving any attention!

We have seen last eight years pass like this in parliamentary chaos. Can we afford to have a non-functional parliament like this for all time to come?

19 December, 2018

IAS Babu and Coal Conviction

All those who take serious interest in the way our country is governed must have noticed the sentencing of 3 senior bureaucrats including the then coal secretary Mr HC Gupta (who was my senior in Muir Hostel, Allahabad University) for two years jail. Our TV channels have somewhat buried this news in the strident sound bites of Kashmir and related patriotism.

UPA II lost the 2014 general elections due to the perception of mammoth scams of which coalgate was one. With 2G scam, it also became an apparent loot of natural resources which the nation watched in disgust. Who was responsible for it? CBI, forced and pushed by the Supreme Court, attempted to find its answer and as a result put up many charge sheets. In one such case this conviction has taken place. Some points in this regard are noticeable:-

- These officers have been punished for putting up false facts of screening committee for the coal blocks before the then coal minister and PM Dr. Manmohan Singh. They did not notice deliberately or negligently facts about the companies and made wrong recommendations to the minister for allotment of the coal blocks.
- Mr H C Gupta enjoyed very good and honest reputation among his colleagues who are shocked by this conviction. However, judicially his fault is proved.
- Top bureaucrats are saying that it would become very difficult for them to take decisions in government for fear of CBI and therefore policy making will become slow. However, this logic should not be used to condone the misdeeds.

- I think the bureaucrats should not be involved in decision-making on economic matters. This should be given to the experts in the fields. This will be safe for babus also.
- Dr Manmohan Singh may not be liable for wrong allotment of coal blocks because he went by the recommendations of the secretary. However, he should have cancelled the allotment of the coal blocks when the facts came in the open. It was done by the Supreme Court.
- Has nation been assured that such looting will not take place in future by making systemic changes ? I don't think so.
- Isn't the conviction in corruption cases taken too lightly in India? After so much of legal tangle if the charges were really proved then only two years of jail seems to be light. In most of the countries, including democratic, punishment would have been far more severe.

24 March, 2017

Vigilance Awareness Week

A few days back, I was invited by the Zonal Manager of Andhra Bank, Bhopal for closing the Vigilance Awareness Week. The Central Vigilance Commission (CVC) had decided that this year the Vigilance Awareness Week would be observed with the theme of the week "My Vision- Corruption Free India".

The observance of the Vigilance Awareness Week has commenced with the Integrity Pledge by the public servants in the Ministries/Departments/Central Public Sector Enterprises (CPSEs)/Public Sector Banks (PSBs) and all other Government Organisations.

The moot issue is that even though these days we are not listening sensational scams at the top, yet at the ground level or say at cutting edge corruption has become almost a way of life. Some people may argue that at this level it might have even increased.

17 November, 2017

Bagpat Incident Police - Law - Society

Last week in Bagpat, UP a young couple was enjoying the fast food at a stall. Suddenly the kins of the girl dragged her lover and started thrashing him. Some onlookers and later a police officer also joined in thrashing before taking him to the police station. The only fault of the youth was that he loved the girl.

The Constitution of India guarantees the right to love to every adult couple and even permits them to live together. Recently a bench of the Supreme Court reiterated this right in unequivocal words. All members of the executive, including police, are supposed to follow the law of the land in letter and spirit. The moot question is that who will protect the couple who wants to use the right to love!

The obvious answer is the police, in case the society fails to protect or becomes hostile to love. In a patriarchal society of western UP, it was a miracle that the lover boy was only beaten and not lynched. I am not surprised with the mindset of the girl's relatives or the mob but I am deeply anguished by the behaviour of the policeman. Was he enforcing the law or was he following the wrong values of the society? So called social moral fabric was guiding him and he ignored the law.

When I entered the IPS in mid seventies the police was very conservative as also were the courts. There was no rape unless the woman was injured or until her bangles were broken. We were assured and also hoped at that time that the modern training and gender sensitisation will inculcate a modern outlook in the police force. Sadly, nothing has changed even after four decades, and the police and to a certain extent the lower judiciary have the same mindset as that of the Bagpat mob. What is the way out?

Can our leaders find the way? No, see the regressive chief ministers of Haryana and Rajasthan and many more leaders who side with Khap mentality for vote bank. Look at the Member of Parliament from this very place Baghpat, a central Minister Satyapal Singh (ex-IPS) who repudiates the theory of Darwin to get conservative Jat votes. Can our Media help? No, see the way the channels played with the honour of Sridevi in death.

I feel, it is high time that leaders of the civil society and the leaders of the police and the judiciary should come forward and wage a relentless war against the rotten traditional views which are oppressive and they should uphold the law of the land which is based on human dignity.

2 March, 2018

Republic Day Parade, 2018

In 1966, as a young boy, I got the opportunity to see the Republic Day parade in New Delhi. Again I saw this parade in 2011 when I was posted in New Delhi.

Like many previous years, this year also I watched the parade on TV. The highlight of this year's parade was the presence of 10 ASEAN heads of state/government. This time the parade was much grander and better organised. It was organised with great thinking and was overall relaxed. The civilian component was as impressive as military. Govt of

India had two audiences in mind to impress- firstly the ten foreign leaders and secondly the people of India.

The military might was clear. India's growing strength on land, air and especially sea along with missiles was visible. Para military contingents did very well. The message to ASEAN was to show that India may be their strategic partner against China.

Women or say daughters of India were highlighted as never before. In all military equipments women were visible. Daredevil BSF Seema Bhawanis performed spectacularly well by their balance on motor bikes.

Display of north-east India was overtly visible. Tripura and Manipur were specially exhibited. Manipur is gateway to Thailand and India is upgrading this road in Myanmar. This highway will open land routes to many ASEAN countries by 2020.

Tableaux were chosen very carefully. It gave emphasis on Govt's agenda on education, agriculture and curbing black money. Again, subtle display of Buddhism, Indonesian style Ramayan and general diversity of India including our north-east was also addressed to foreign chief guests.

Children and especially girls' cultural programmes were very colourful and meaningful. Congratulations to Ministry of Defence which is the main organiser and to Delhi Police and DD for their excellent performance.

26 January, 2018

Efficacy of Parliament

The country had a sigh of relief when the current monsoon session of the parliament ended with some legislative work. Except for triple talaq and motor vehicle bills, the government was able to get other important bills passed by both houses of the parliament. The bill to provide punch to prevention of atrocities on SC and ST and one for conferring constitutional status on Backward Castes Commission were passed without any resistance.

The present decade will be a black chapter in the constitutional history of India. Stalling the proceedings of the parliament has become almost a routine. The idea behind stalling the proceedings is that the government of the day should not be permitted to do a good job. Opposition does not like any good legislation which will give credit to the government. If the nation suffers, it is none of the concern of the opposition political parties.

It all started during the period of UPA II. BJP blocked the parliament on the issue of 2G scam of colossal magnitude (but the case surprisingly later ended in a meek acquittal). Sushma Swaraj in Lok Sabha and Arun Jaitely in Rajya Sabha then propounded the theory of blocking of the house. Sushma Swaraj, then leader of opposition in the Lok Sabha, had declared that "not allowing Parliament to function is also a form of democracy, like any other form". With this dangerous philosophy BJP kept, session after session, the parliament in a state of impairment on the pretext of shocking scams. This rendered the lacklustre government of Manmohan Singh totally paralytic. The bills of far reaching significance like GST and Aadhar were not allowed to be passed by the BJP. The nation suffered.

The polls of 2014 saw with dismay a decimated Congress with 44 seats in Lok Sabha. BJP or NDA, with huge majority started with exuberance implementing their agenda of legislation. However, soon they discovered a very painful Rajya Sabha, where UPA had clear majority. Congress took the revenge with vengeance and stalled all attempts to pass legislation for reform of land and labour laws. The country had great hopes to achieve growth rates of Chinese scale with these reforms, but Congress dashed these hopes. In a condescending gesture, Congress allowed passage of Bills on Aadhar, GST and Bankruptcy.

We Indians are very proud of our democracy, and rightly so. Our Supreme Court jealously guards the rights of individuals. But our foremost pillar of democracy, Parliament has degenerated into a wretched arena of highly partisan politics. Any opposition will oppose a bill of great benefit to the people only to deny the possible goodwill for the ruling party. Our MPs are most arrogant, undisciplined and callous politicians in the world, after Pakistan. It is a miracle that India is the fastest growing economy but in my opinion it is not because of the politicians but due to the efforts of the industrious people of India.

13 August, 2018

Message From Kathua and Unnao Rape Cases

These two rape cases have badly shaken the conscience of the country. After the gruesome Nirbhaya rape case, the attention of the country has now been drawn by the media to these inhuman incidents.

In Kathua incident local schism between local Hindus and poor but liberal wandering Muslim Shepherds was the instigating factor. This went to the limits of this horrendous crime being perpetrated on an eight year old innocent girl. The communal angle of this crime manifested itself in old fault lines between Jammu and Kashmir regions. In Unnao MLA of Bangarmau, his brother and henchmen, who have criminal background in this rural constituency, committed offences of rape and murder.

In both these cases ruling BJP tried to shield the accused. BJP wants to show its supporters that it can save them even in heinous crimes. Its middle level leadership defended the culprits but now it shrewdly tells its supporters that it is helpless in defending them under pressure of media and courts.

Initial role of police in these cases is well known— they sought guidance from political rulers or were instructed by the rulers to defend the accused. However, it is to the credit of J&K Crime Branch to come out with good investigation. The lawyer community of Jammu behaved in a shameless communal manner. UP police who boasts of encounters of criminals was at the feet of the accused MLA. The DG and the CM were relieved that the case has been handed over to the CBI and that they have not to arrest the MLA.

Modi, as usual, at long last broke his silence and said words of wisdom of giving justice to victims. Yogi after defying for long by not arresting the criminal MLA handed over the case to the CBI and said the same hypocritical nice words. V K Singh was first senior Minister to offer words of solace to the victims' families. Suddenly women politicians also came forward to give statements. Smriti Irani called for action against the culprits while Menka Gandhi came out with the same old idea of capital punishment in child rape cases. A country which gets nervous in hanging terrorist like Afzal Guru is called for hanging the rapists. In India, only one in six rapes is reported and out of them only a quarter are punished. A comic relief came from a political light weight, Nand Kumar Chauhan who saw Pakistani hands in Kathua. He does not even know the difference between Jammu and Kashmir.

Congress in the beginning kept silence weighing the vote bank consequences. Finally, Congress decided to attack from the front and Rahul Gandhi decided to light the candles at the famous India Gate. Does Congress remember that Rahul Gandhi was invisible and conspicuous by absence during Nirbhaya uproar? Congress also owes an explanation to the nation for not making an impartial police system after independence. It maintained the colonial system and even further made the police helpless before the ruling politicians. The gutless and unscrupulous policemen buckle down at the first sign of political pressure. Can't India have a police which is impartial and works efficiently without political manipulation? But alas not a single political party in India wants a responsible and impartial police system. When in power they misuse it for their interest and when in opposition they shout loudly against police. Together they never think of police reforms.

Even with the best of police there would be cases like Kathua and Unnao, but at least public would have had faith in police investigation and the wheels of justice would have rolled without encumbrances leaving our conscience intact!

14 April, 2018

Ram Rahim & Law (And Order)

Ram Rahim, a self proclaimed saint, has been held guilty of rape and therefore he is a criminal. But bigger criminals are his supporters who are mercilessly destroying property in the name of spirituality.

Things went out of hands once the court's judgement was pronounced. 28 people are reported to have been killed along with large scale and widespread violence.

It is strange that High Court asked the police to use force as if police requires orders of the HC for this. The Court was probably right because it saw that police was only mobilising forces and not taking any effective preventive action. The CM, administration and the police followed the path of least resistance hoping for a happy ending. This meant disaster.

Mr Khattar, CM Haryana, has already proved his utter incompetence in earlier agitations especially in Jat agitation. We saw lot of property being destroyed without any resistance from the police. The gutless politicians in power allow the mobs to plunder, arson and violence.

It is also time for social and religious leaders to ponder as to why a goon like Ram Rahim comes to acquire so much of clout and befool the gullible supporters.

25 August, 2017

The Roman Praetorian Guards -and Indian Police

The senior advocate of Supreme Court, Rana Mukherjee submitted his views in a study circle on the topic 'Limits of Interference of the Constitutional Courts in Police Investigations'. Among other things, he compared the Indian Police with Roman Praetorian Guards in arbitrariness. My comments are as under:-

The problem with the Indian police is that it is totally under the clutches of the political executive. The present Police Act was given to India in 1861 by the Britishers and the sole object of this Act was the preservation of the colonial British Empire. Nearly at the same time England created a different police model for itself, under which the police was strictly under law and not under any executive authority.

In India, courts have been given the responsibility to preserve and protect the fundamental rights of citizens. Therefore, it is inevitable that the courts will interfere with every case of highhandedness including in the police investigation. As only the high and mighty can easily approach the constitutional courts, the courts have to be selective in their interference in the matters which are brought before it. We have seen that many activists and those who run NGOs have been getting relief (may be rightly) from the courts and at times even without filing a formal petition. Here the crucial point is that the interference by the courts has hardly changed the attitude of the police in the vast interior areas of the country.

The Roman Praetorian Guards was a professional body working not under law but sadly under the tight control of the emperor or sometimes a person with parallel centre of power, who misused them for their vested interests. Similarly, in India police - even though a part of the criminal judicial system - is always treated as the executive wing of the government. Therefore, it is not surprising that it is always being misused by the politicians. Even the opposition parties do not mind the misuse of police by the ruling politicians and only wait for their own turn. Again nowhere in the democratic world police is under the tight control of the bureaucracy. The third National Law Commission (Dharmaveer Commision) had given far-reaching recommendations to improve the police system and suggested to give complete autonomy to the police to carry out their work, with very stringent provisions in case of any misuse of power by them. In other words they were given independence in their working but with a strong supervisory judicial system for redressal of grievances against the police. Almost all the recommendations of the National Police Commission were thrown into dustbin by the Parliament because the politicians are not interested in 'good' police but they are interested only in their 'own' police whom they use at times shamelessly from villages to Metropolitan cities.

Politicians also ignore misconducts of the police in lieu of loyalty.

In my opinion a rational and law abiding police will not leave any scope for constitutional courts to interfere in its investigative role. This interference is not really practical or desirable because of their very nature and limitation, the constitutional courts can only be selective and can never supervise vast police machinery in a large country.

11 October, 2018

Change in Policing

In the picture I am at the laptop presenting my work on the proposed changes in some important Minor Criminal Acts and MP Police Regulations. This job was given to me by the Atal Bihari Vajpayee Institute of Good Governance, MP Govt.

Here I am presenting my work before the Government and the Police representatives and experts. Feeling happy to finish a tedious work. It is for the government now to act or not to act on my recommendations.

9 March, 2016

My Alma Mater, Lucknow University

Rain Forest of Temburong, Brunei

Chapter - 11

Nature is Soul

Season's March

I peeped out of my window this evening when shadows were lengthening, but had not faded into the darkness. A slow and steady march of the season to replicate recurrent

moments in nature is now discernible. With winter panting to keep pace, traces of change and yellowness in landscape are trying to assert.

What else is eternity?

18 February, 2018

The Nearest Mars

I took this picture of Mars last night. Mars is closest to the earth tonight after 15 years. In the picture you can see a bright little spot in the middle which is Mars. It is at a distance of 5 crore 76 lakh km from the earth at this time.

Mars is the fourth planet from the Sun and first on the outer side of earth. It is the second smallest planet in the Solar System after Mercury. Interestingly Mars has the tallest mountains in the solar system. The surface of Mars has an orange or reddish colour because its soil has iron oxide or rust particles in it. The sky on Mars often appears pink or light orange, because the dust in the soil is blown into Mars' thin atmosphere by winds.

1 August, 2018

A Visit to Jungle

Forests have been my passion since my early age. Once inside woods, I always feel a transcendental change in me. This passion has taken me to different national parks of India-from Kashmir to Kerala and from Manipur to Gujarat. This passion also took me to Africa and North America. Yesterday I got an opportunity to visit Rajaji National Park, Uttarakhand.

Just at the entrance of the park I got the glimpses of the Himalayas. I took this picture from the dry bed of the river Mohand on the border of the districts Saharanpur (UP) and

Haridwar (Uttarakhand). The Gangetic plains of India move northward to touch the feet of the Himalayas. The small hillocks in the picture are the beginning of the Himalayas called the Shivalik ranges. This is the end of the Gangetic plains and the rise of the great Himalayas. Further I reached at Beriwara forest rest house constructed in 1882, and surprisingly situated in the middle of thick forest of this National Park.

This forest covers an area of 820 sq km in the districts of Dehradun, Haridwar and Pauri of Uttarakhand. It is situated between the Shivalik ranges and the Indo-Gangetic plains. Broad-leaved deciduous forests, riparian vegetation, scrubland, grasslands and pine forests are found in this park. The beautiful dense jungles here are home to vivacious wildlife. Varying topography makes it a cradle for wide variety of wildlife. Though called a Tiger Reserve, I was fascinated here by elephants, leopards, all varieties of antelopes, birds and above all its natural beauty.

26 May, 2019

Planet Venus

I took the picture of the planet Venus, which shines the brightest these nights after sunset up to around 10 pm over Bhopal sky. You can easily spot it by looking to North West with more West (293 WNW) at a low height. Looking to Venus you can also see fairly visible star Capella slightly on the right hand side (311 WN), and comparatively bright star Sirius on the left hand side (235 SW).

Enjoy the night sky in lockdown. However, one can see only a few stars even in these dark nights, because of the heavy glow of light of the city.

21 April, 2020

Black Panther Saya and His Lady Love Cleopatra

Sometime back, I read a news-item about a black panther Saya and his lady love, leopardess Cleopatra. They are living happily in the jungle of Kabini. I became fascinated with this stunning pair and this led me to probe more about them.

Kabini forest is situated between the two districts of Mysore and Kodagu in the state of Karnataka. The national park stretches at the foothills of the Western Ghats spreading down the Brahmagiri hills and south towards Kerala state. River Kabini separates this forest from the Bandipur National Park.

Saya was born black. Saya is black because his skin has too much of melanin- a substance which also makes the skin of human beings dark. Saya was very proud of his colour, and for this pride, he was hounded by his species out of a large territory of the forest. He was denied access to ladies. However, there was Cleopatra, a blonde and beautiful leopardess, who passionately fell in love with Saya. She deserted her partner and came with Saya, without fearing the violent reprisal of the old associates. Saya and Cleopatra roam together in their own small territory. Both are together since they met long time back- something which is very uncommon among family- panthera.

I wish all the best to this couple.

12 September, 2020

Rain Forest

Rain forests are the densest forest with the tallest trees. I and Laxmi went to Temburong forests in north Borneo. It was a very tough and physically challenging journey. After 15 km of normal ferry boat we reached Bangar, and then started in a long boat for 12 km. Long boat manoeuvred precariously in the fast current of the river with sharp gradient and with stony shallows and whirling depths. The clime on the forest hill was very difficult with about 1000 steps with some hanging bridges. However, the top of the clime was a reward of joy with a 360 degree view of a majestic expanse of forests from over the canopy of the trees.

21 August, 2019

Chapter - 12

Justice from Courts

Judiciary And Its Bickerings

As a person who has risked his life in defending country and its constitution, I am pained by the press conference by four seniormost judges of the Supreme Court (SC). What they said in a very guarded language was to bring out the reality of the functioning of the SC by pointing out the poor administration of the SC and malfunctioning of the CJI. In effect they said that the CJI is allotting important cases to his favourite benches of judges for certain reasons. This idea is very chilling as judiciary is the last place of hope for citizens in personal disputes and more importantly, for the proper functioning of all parts of the state.

However, all this we knew beforehand. It was no revelation to us. Four judges only exposed it from inside. In my opinion judges, though true on substance, adopted a controversial mode of airing their grievances of judiciary. Press conference in long run will set a disturbing precedent. This is not acceptable. These judges could have aired their views in the judgement in any relevant case or in a PIL.

Imagine what will happen to the army and the nation if at the time of war four Lt. Generals hold a press conference on some correct issue against the army chief. If the SC defends our liberties, the military defends our very existence as a nation.

We all know that in March 1973, Indira Gandhi gave a body blow to judicial independence by superseding three SC judges to appoint AN Ray as CJI who was considered to be pro Government. SC took a lot of time to recover this assault. The higher judiciary is an important and unique institution. It is fully autonomous and accountable only to itself. At times it is perceived to be arbitrary and especially in many instances with no transparent method for dealing with the corruption in judiciary. It has appropriated for itself the constitution for the appointment of judges by giving an opaque system of collegium.

It is imperative for the judiciary to constantly assess itself in a just and discrete way for its own functioning. The stakes of the nations in the judiciary are very high.

13 January, 2018

Lalu in Soup

I appreciate the courage of the CBI judge of Jharkhand who sentenced Lalu for seven and seven years of consecutive imprisonment. This means he has to serve 14 years in jail. Normally Indian judiciary is heavily tilted towards accused in trial by giving benefit of doubt, and if at all proved guilty then in awarding light punishment. This is the ethos of our jurisprudence borrowed from England. In some respect it is even more tilted towards accused than what it is in England, for example, Section 25 of the Evidence Act regarding non-admissibility of statement in India of the accused before the police.

Our courts avoid giving maximum punishment for any offence for one reason or the other and such situation is when our very few cases are proved in the courts. The cases fail because of the enormous delay in trial of cases and typical habit of Indian witnesses to turn hostile in the courts, and also due to the lack of scientific evidence by the police.

There is a public perception that even where lower courts have given sufficient punishment, the High Courts and Supreme Court reduce the punishment or altogether acquit the accused. Also when the accused is punished under different Acts or under different sections of the same Act, the punishments are awarded simultaneously.

In this situation, the punishment awarded to Lalu is exemplary. He has been sentenced to seven years in IPC and seven years in Prevention of Corruption Act. Both sentences will be consecutive i.e. one after the other. But there is one technical relief for Lalu and that is the long delay in disposal of appeals. His first conviction of five years has been challenged in appeal and that is still pending and he got bail. Now, Lalu is convicted in three more cases and is facing one more case. Lalu may appeal in High Court and Supreme Court and may get bail pending appeal. If that happens, then he may not fight election but still influence politics as a champion of secularism and social justice.

However, this punishment is well deserved and may hopefully deter other politicians not to become absolutely brazen in corruption.

24 March, 2018

Salman The Convict

Feelings are divided over the five years imprisonment of Salman Khan for poaching. For some, it is very harsh punishment. Many of such people feel that Salman should not have been punished at all. Many in the film industry are worried about the investment involved in Salman's films. Again there are large number of his fans for whom it is very painful and they wonder whether there is anything wrong in poaching a blackbuck. After all, it is a sport of fun and Salman is too great a humanitarian person to be punished for such a trivial matter.

There are, on the other side, people like crazy Bishnois who sometimes love animals more than human beings. They are rejoicing over the court verdict. There are people who by their very basic nature are hostile to high and mighty and they may get some pleasure in this judgement.

Rule of law is a concept at the core of the democracy and equality is its biggest tenet. However, when it comes to judicial system it seems to favour the rich. They can take the help of the best legal brains and exploit all the procedural webs. They can file endless appeals and petitions, if the delay suits them. They can also expedite the justice whenever it is required. Look at the fast speed, where in a few hours Bombay High Court granted bail to Salman, after he was punished by the session court in the hit and run case.

The present case of 1998 has been inordinately delayed. It was a simple case of poaching. It took six years to frame charges against the accused persons. Next seven years were wasted in higher courts for procedural objections. The real trial started in 2013 and verdict came in five years. This verdict will now be challenged in High Court and Supreme Court and may take unknown time to reach its logical end. Salman may also be acquitted. Meanwhile the convict may get bail and resume his films, where huge investments are at stake.

Today a common man may feel relieved that our courts, sometimes, deliver real justice because a large number of cases end up in acquittal due to delayed trial, poor investigation and prosecution and above all dishonesty of our witnesses and law enforcers. As for now, the case of Salman has ended in conviction.

5 April, 2018

Death for Child Rapists

Finally, Government of India through an ordinance made provisions today in the law for death penalty for the rapist of any child below 12. This was a direct knee jerk response to many such cases coming to light and especially highlighted Kathua case. The purpose is to mollify the anger of public and to blunt the opposition's assault. Clearly the purpose is political and for short term gains. However, laws are made for generations, and it is in this perspective that I will briefly mention its implications:-

1. The idea is that death penalty will be a deterrence to the potential culprit of child rape. Needless to say, it is both a fallacy as well as a farce. Every criminal assesses the certainty of the punishment rather than the quantum of it. In the first place, he knows that very few victims dare report the cases due to the sense of shame and secondly, if at all they report them chances of conviction are very little due to slow legal system. We must make punishment certain and fast in every case to deter the culprit.
2. The new law says that death penalty may be awarded. It is not mandatory. Indian legal tradition is to award capital punishment only in the rarest of the rare cases. As child rapes are being reported so often, then most such cases would not be the rarest of the rare cases.
3. We should know that majority of all rapes including child rapes are within the family and are normally not reported. It is estimated that only one in six cases

is reported. It renders any change in law meaningless for the unreported cases.

4. Police lacks skill and scientific resources to investigate the cases. The overworked, tired and demotivated police does the minimum possible enquiry, which may be just sufficient for the challan. There is no reward or punishment to policemen in any investigative work because their career depend only upon the pleasure of politicians. The state governments led by any political party have thrown the police reforms and Supreme Court's directives into the dustbin.
5. After investigation the case goes to the committal court and sessions court where it is argued by government pleader who is a political appointee. He is mostly incompetent and frequently corrupt. Against him pitted are the far superior lawyers of the accused.
6. Courts are burdened with huge pendency. Inordinate delay in trial gives opportunity to the accused for manipulation of witnesses. There is genuine demand for the fast track courts for rape cases but so is the demand for SC/ST Act cases, corruption cases and murder cases etc. What we require is an entire fast track judiciary. Unfortunately, no politician is interested in it because some of them are themselves criminals and want very slow moving courts.

With these constraints, with the passage of time even propaganda value of death penalty in child rape will wane.

24 April, 2018

Congestion in Courts

Supreme Court harshly reprimanded the Central Government for filing mindlessly appeals after appeals, and that too, in bunches. The Central Government had filed appeals in such cases in which earlier appeals were quashed by the Court. The government also paid lavishly on the battery of lawyers. The Court has the constitutional luxury of reprimanding anyone under the sky. This time the Court has rightly raised the point that the Government is clogging the cases and choking the drains of justice.

I wanted to write about it but drifted in many other happenings. Today Times of India reminded me by an editorial. The Court had gone literary and termed it RIP Van Winkleism, an idiom which is derived from a person who slept a lot and ignored prudence.

I am reminded of that when I was Additional Secretary in the Home Department of MP, one DSP went to High Court and rightly got extra seniority in service. Exactly on similar facts many DSPs applied for extra seniority and I recommended for them. I was shocked when a babu of GAD said that every DSP has to go separately to High Court and get his order. His view was endorsed by my superiors. Eventually all such DSPs got their due seniority only through the court.

Forget about central and state governments even Nagar Nigams (Municipal Corporations) are also going to Supreme Court very frequently and throwing money on litigations which could have been used in cleaning the junk. In the police department opinions in many cases used to be sought from prosecutors about the suitability of the case to be put up before the court even on very weak evidence. The prosecutors routinely used to write 'The evidence in the case is very weak, however the case should be put up in the court for disposal.' Invariably such cases ended in acquittal. On the contrary, in Japan even if a criminal case is proved in investigation, the prosecution may refuse to prosecute it if it finds that the case is frivolous and will waste the time of the court.

Much has been said about pendency in the courts and various steps which may be taken to reduce it. I don't want to go into the details but will point out that more and more demands for fast track courts for different types of heinous offences are being raised, meaning thereby that other cases are not important. I had been emphasising that we must think sincerely to expedite the entire judicial process, for which many pertinent recommendations are already available.

2 May, 2018

Constitution and the Recent Happenings

India is fortunate to have a constitution which was drafted by a galaxy of brilliant persons who were also men of integrity. They understood the complexity of India, and they were also well versed with the western concept of equality, liberty and justice. They had closely watched the working of the states in different parts of the world and gifted us a constitution which has taken roots by now.

Our constitution has withstood the vagaries of communal, regional and petty social and political forces. Three pillars of the state have successfully checked and balanced each other. With lack of political will on several non vote-bank issues, our parliament has not brought much far-reaching changes in the society. The Supreme Court, not scared of vote-bank, has usually been bolder than the legislature.

Gradually the Supreme Court has come to know that our parliament is gutless and very weak due to extremely narrow political interests. In all these decades the parliament could not scrutinise the old and archaic pre-independence laws and statutes in the light of the constitution. This work should have been done immediately after the independence. It was only Nehru who tried for modern reforms and got

Hindu Code Bill passed. He, however, did not try for common civil code which was envisaged in the constitution. India at that time would have accepted common civil code. This would have given India a social harmony that all civilised societies have.

Supreme Court has started giving verdicts on politically (and for some morally) controversial issues like entry into places of worship, triple talaq, harshness of SC/ST (POA) Act, homosexuality and adultery etc. In a traditional country where a vast majority is still not educated in real sense, obscurantists of all shades in different religions, castes and sects will not reconcile to the liberal and modern outlook of our constitution. No wonder in many regards RSS and AIMPLB look alike.

Supreme Court, though not strictly meant for it, is somewhat inadvertently liberating India from medieval values. Credit does not solely go to the Supreme Court, but also to the forefathers of the constitution who created such institution.

8 September, 2018

Judicial Verdict on Ayodhya Dispute

A five judge bench of the Supreme Court of India, headed by the CJI, has unanimously decided the civil appeal numbers 10866 and 10867 of 2010. It was no ordinary civil case. It was the most emotive and contentious issue ever decided by the Supreme Court in its history. The judgement runs into 1045 pages, and I read only as many as interested me. In the dispute was a plot of 2.77 acres situated in the heart of Ayodhya. In an area of 0.33 acre of this plot, once there stood a mosque named after the first Moghul conqueror of large tracts of North India. This disputed land is of immense significance for both Hindus and Muslims. Hindus claim that this is the place where Lord Ram was born. Ram is not only religiously sacrosanct for Hindus but He is an inseparable part of spiritual, social and cultural ethos of Hindus. Even the dead, being carried for cremation, have to listen to the chants of His name. For Muslims, this was a mosque which was first desecrated in 1949 and then demolished in 1992. They have a feeling of victimhood.

The Supreme Court had to decide this case on very sketchy evidence, which at times is on the verge of conjectures. The undisputed fact is that there was an ordinary looking mosque built in 1528 by Mir Baqi, a general of Babar. Namaz was offered here till 1949. On the other hand, Hindus claim that they have an unbroken tradition of worshipping at this place as birthplace of Ram. The year 1856 is a landmark, as only after this year the evidence is documented and facts are clear. But before that the evidence is blurred. At the outset the court declares that they will decide the case only on evidence and not on faith. The court has very extensively explored the evidence and found it in favour of Hindus. They looked at the old scriptures, archaeological evidence, some travelogues of European visitors, old available official records and oral testimony of the witnesses. On archaeological information, the court has inferred that there was some non-Islamic structure under the mosque but no temple was demolished for its construction. The Court mentions Tieffenthaler's account wherein in 1740 he makes a reference of Hindu devotees. The Court quotes the report of Carnegy, Assistant Commissioner, Faizabad who mentions in 1860s about the Hindu traditions. The Court concludes, "that the consistent pattern of Hindus worship including the making of offerings to the Garbh Grih while standing at the railing, there can be no manner of doubt that this was in furtherance of their belief that the birthplace of Lord Ram was within the precincts of and under the central dome of the mosque".

The Muslims were in possession of the inner courtyard but the outer courtyard was always in possession of the Hindus. Even the inner courtyard was contested by the Hindus, and Muslims have produced no evidence to indicate that their possession of the disputed structure was exclusive and that offering of namaz was exclusionary of Hindus. The Court says that Hindus and Muslims had a competing right over the disputed site but Hindus showed better evidence of their continuous worship at the disputed structure for centuries. Muslims also failed to establish their ownership through adverse possession. The court has gone by preponderance of evidence and better probability. It says "On the balance of probabilities the evidence in respect of the possessory claim of the Hindus to the composite whole of the disputed property stands on a better footing than the evidence adduced by the Muslims". The court finally handed over the disputed plot to the Hindus. Invoking Article 142 of the Constitution the court has granted 5 acres of land to the Muslims for the construction of a new mosque.

In the name of the 'full faith' in judiciary a large number of political and social leaders have hailed the decision of the court. The majority of Muslims is also reconciled with the judgement of the apex court. Some critics of the judgement feel that the verdict has rewarded violence. I quote one journalist who has lashed out "in its own way it is a judgement on the New India, an India where the Supreme Court has judged that reason has no place any longer". Another has hit out "The high- minded secular rhetoric of the judgement is dislocated from the majoritarian edge in its ruling". I think in a vibrant democracy, we must accept that there is place for such criticism. This case was so complicated that any judgement would have evoked some dissent. My take on this verdict is that a matter which had divided the two communities for centuries has finally found 'some' solution. All Indians including minorities must accept it in the interest of the harmony of our great nation and wholeheartedly declare that the issue of Ram Janam Bhumi and Babri Masjid is finally settled. We have to move forward.

19 November, 2019

Chapter - 13

Persons of Eminence

Lee Kuan Yew

The great leader of Asia, Lee Kuan Yew is no more. He built modern Singapore which today is an object of envy even for rich or well governed countries. He had before him a city state to develop which was like mini India of different religions and peoples. With tough discipline, hard work and welfare of all communities, he made Singapore a world class city.

Writing about him, *New York Times* wrote that China is working on the path of Lee on a bigger land. The paper also mentions about Modi's India Swachcha Bharat Abhiyan and hints that probably he may improve India.

The paper fears that too much of democracy may hinder India's growth. For quite a lot of us democracy means criticising everything and doing nothing. We are happy the way we are!

24 March, 2015

Maulana Abul Kalam Azaad

- First Education Minister of India

Recently my one respected senior officer drew my attention to a video in which there was vilification of the character of Maulana Abul Kalam Azaad. He is described as uneducated man, who spoiled the education of India. He is also said to have done nothing for the independence movement. I will not like to forward the video but the factual position as I mentioned to my senior officer is as under:-

> "Sir, I heard the video. Many selective facts which the speaker gives in the video are correct but his assessment of Maulana's personality is awfully distorted".

The father of Maulana Azaad was a Bengali of Afghan descent (Afghans were the rulers of Bengal in medieval time). However, his father lived in Delhi and shifted to Mecca in 1857, due to turmoil in Delhi. His father was also a prolific writer. He married a woman from Medina. He died early and Maulana Azaad, born in Mecca in 1888, returned to Calcutta with the family at the age of two years. He was home- schooled by several able tutors. Let us remember that even Tagore had schooling at home. Azaad was a brilliant student and he started writing articles at the age of 14 and brought out a journal at the age of 15. He can be called a precocious child. He extensively studied world history, mathematics, theology, philosophy and languages. He was fluent in Arabic and knew many languages. At the age of 17 he opposed the partition of Bengal on communal line by Lord Curzon in 1905. That partition laid the foundation of future East Pakistan. Azaad also associated himself with the revolutionaries of Bengal.

In 1919, he joined the Khilafat movement launched by Mahatma Gandhi. This movement was against the abolition of Islamic Khalifat system situated in Turkey. This movement brought him in touch with Gandhi ji and he became his devout disciple throughout his life. He was one of the founders of Jamia Millia Islamia during British time, first at

Aligarh and then at Delhi. He participated with full vigour in all the movements launched by Mahatma Gandhi and was also jailed. From the beginning, he was a known opponent of Muslim League. He was the president of the Congress party in 1923–24 and again in turbulent period of 1940–46. He opposed the partition of India to the best of his ability. He became very close to Nehru. During partition, he was looking after the safety of Indian Muslims. There was no Muslim leader taller than him who believed in non-violence and secularism.

He was a great scholar and a very extensive writer. He was a great theologian and interpreted many Islamic books and yet he was a committed secularist. He wrote books on philosophy and wrote articles on many subjects. As education minister his focus was on universal education, especially rural education for boys and girls. Keeping pace with Nehru, Maulana Azaad also had a scientific temper. As early as 1951, he established IIT Kharagpur. I have myself visited Kharagpur and I have seen his influence there. He also encouraged and helped the Indian Institute of Science, Bangalore.

Congress party was like a huge banyan tree, where there were Muslim scholar like Maulana Azaad and staunch Hindu like Madan Mohan Malviya. They all had one common thing and that was the total adherence to the ideals of Mahatma Gandhi.

In my esteem Maulana Azaad was one of the greatest stalwarts whom India should be proud of. It is to the credit of Narasimha Rao that he awarded Maulana Azaad 'Bharat Ratna' in 1992.

12 October, 2020

Abhijit Banerjee Gets Nobel Memorial Prize

Abhijit Banerjee along with his French American wife Esther Duflo and Michael Kremer was awarded Nobel Memorial Prize for 2019 in Economic Sciences. It's a great honour for India and I personally feel thrilled about it.

What fascinates me about this economist is that he is solely devoted to the study of poverty, and its alleviation by different interventions. India has been in his focus. He has studied in depth various government schemes meant for poverty alleviation in India and globally.

A few years back, I had a chance to come across his book- *Poor Economics*. This had an innovative research based study on field experiments. He has shown how the problem of global poverty can be tackled by breaking it down into a number of smaller but more precise questions at individual or group levels.

Coming to the Indian context, Banerjee is sceptical about the present Indian economic situation. He was against the demonetisation. He claims that presently Indian economy is on a shaky ground with no assurance for revival. An alumni of Presidency College, Calcutta and an activist of JNU, he is a darling of Congress party and the Left. Watch out! BJP will be wary of him.

14 October, 2019

Hillary Clinton - in India

Hillary Clinton spoke today in India Today Conclave. I was impressed by her forthright and clear ideas which she put forth very succinctly. She was in India, but she was conscious that she is being heard globally. She openly attacked Putin and his Russian aggressions. She minced no words in condemning Putin for hacking emails and leaking it to undermine her election.

She assailed Trump vehemently, both personally and politically. She talked about Trump having gone bankrupt four times and for having very little authentic information. He has undone international commitments of US, especially in Trans Pacific trade and climate change etc. She said that Democrats would try to control the House of Representatives to check the president. She alleged that Trump has divided American society on racial ground. He only loves authoritarian leaders.

She attacked Pakistan for helping terrorists. She took credit to advise Obama to raid Osama bin Laden in Pakistan. She praised India for its democracy and wanted it to take leadership in the world affairs.

She was not only putting political points but giving detailed backgrounds of her convictions and philosophy - something we find missing in Indian leaders. Of late, Modi and Rahul attack each other on foreign soil and in my opinion there is nothing wrong in this, because we are a democratic country and our leaders should carry that ethos everywhere. But unlike Hillary, Modi and Rahul both lack the academic depth and strength of conviction when they attack each other. They do so for their narrow political ends and are not bothered about analysing the socio-political forces of this country. Hillary put her intellectual discourse with ease.

Hillary's emphasis on democratic values, pluralism and anti-divisive policy should serve as a pointer to Modi and India.

11 March, 2018

Meghan Markle- a Remarkable Woman

(Now Duchess of Sussex)

Meghan Markle, 37 years old ex-actress of Hollywood is a daughter of a black African American and an American father of European descent. She grew in Hollywood and was educated in North Western University where she did her double major in Theatre and International Studies.

What is remarkable is that she is a very talented woman. She worked in many TV shows, short and full films, including famous movie *Remember Me*.

She released a line for women's fashion workwear. She was editor in chief of a lifestyle website and worked as lifestyle blogger. She can also write well. Her assets are $ 5 million.

She is a woman of charity and she travelled to many countries for different causes including Rwanda and Afghanistan. She also came to India for feminists cause. She worked for various issues among others from clean drinking water to stigmatisation of menstrual health of women.

After a long relationship with an actor producer Trevor Engelson she married him in 2011 but divorced in 2013. She agreed to the proposal of Prince Harry and became Duchess of Sussex. Rest all is in news papers.

22 May, 2018

Homage to Atal Soul

(Picture: Year 2000, Gwalior)

I pay my heart- felt homage to the departed soul of Atal Bihari Vajpayee. He was not only a great prime minister, but also a towering parliamentarian, a democratic and patriotic statesman, a gifted poet, an effective synthesiser, a

man of steely determination and sharp intellect and above all a fine and beloved human being.

His voice will reverberate for generations to inspire the spirits of less favoured to carve out a new destiny. In the dark night, made darker by clouds, you will still be the lone red planet of hope, like it shines today in the smoke of your five elements.

17 August, 2018

The Tallest Statue

Sardar Patel was not the tallest leader of the 20th century India. As we all know the tallest leader of not only 20th century but for several centuries was Mahatma Gandhi. However, we (the Government) have made the tallest statue (182 m) of Sardar Patel. The tallest statue of Mahatma in the world is only 22 m in Patna.

No one can deny the importance of Sardar Patel in unifying over 550 princely states of India. But in all fairness to Sardar Patel, we can say that he was an important front ranking leaders who could have been probably a suitable candidate for the first Prime Minister. However, anyone who is well-versed with the history of India of a few years before and after the independence will admit that Sardar Patel wielded authority which was almost equal to Nehru.

Because of the liberal and Fabian socialistic ideas, Nehru was far more popular among the intellectuals and the writers. In the light of the Nehruvian thought, many other outstanding and brilliant leaders who had done extreme sacrifice (except perhaps Ambedkar) could not find their due place in the Indian world of ideas. However, there was a sizeable section of scholars and common people who also had admiring perspectives for other leaders of India. BJP is trying to exploit the sentiments of this section of Indians who also admire leaders other than Nehru.

We have to see in future how many more statues of other leaders of this size or even taller are installed on the skyline of India!

31 October, 2018

Mahatma - 150th Birthday

Mohandas Karamchand Gandhi, whom millions of Indians in reverence fondly called Mahatma Gandhi, was one of the tallest persons ever born in India. He not only fought against the mighty British Empire with highly principled moral means, but also ushered his people to an enlightened social upliftment. He propounded the Indian ethos by following the principles of truth and non-violence. He championed the cause of women and downtrodden and always empathised with the most deprived human being. He fought against the British but loved the English people. His spiritual strength gave him a rare compassion to love the entire humanity. He was fearless because his strength came from the purest inner self. His message is universal and will remain a guiding light for the humanity for centuries to come.

I join the nation in bowing my head in memory of this great soul on his 150th birthday.

1 October, 2019

Chapter - 14

Education is Light

Educating India

It was a pleasant experience to witness the results of CBSE classes 12 and 10. 83.01% students in class 12 and 86.7% in class 10 have passed in these examinations. It is very heartening to know that like the past once again girls have outshone the boys. Out of 11.8 lakh students in class XII CBSE, 72599 have scored more than 90% marks. The better private schools and better funded central schools form the backbone of the CBSE system. These bright girls and students will take the best Indian higher educational institutions like Delhi University, IITs and AIIMS etc. Added to these students are 10 million more from state boards at the same level and only a few of the talented students among them will make up to the best educational institutions. However, India has also to think about the rest of the students!

India has a long tradition of having some good public (which means private) schools and there had been a sudden spurt in their numbers in recent decades. The UPA I passed an RTE Act by which private schools are obliged to take students belonging to the weaker sections. The state governments across India have provided extremely poor standard of free primary education. Their infrastructure is horribly poor and teachers are used to absenteeism and indiscipline. A survey by ASAR has left all the state governments abashed. No wonder that half of urban and one-third of rural children attend private schools. There is also surfeit of cheap private schools (they call themselves Convent) which cater to the needs of the poor masses. The state governments which are not able to manage their own schools are closing down these poor private schools on the uncanny logic of these schools not meeting the official norms.

The students who pass out from class 12 are bewildered for higher education. There are various layers of students and it becomes difficult to provide them appropriate higher education. Some of them want the world class education while on other extreme many want somehow to get only a degree for livelihood. Unlike the school education where system of private schools is firmly established, private participation in higher education is only recently taking roots. Earlier private institutions were far and few but now more and more private universities and other institutions are coming up.

The governments by their very nature of looking into short term vista, are unable or unwilling to comprehend the complex problem of providing quality higher education in this big country. Any long term concept of creating high class centres of higher education is too much to expect from the fast changing governments. Even UGC has throttled the private initiative by enforcing the archaic wooden standards of only measuring the class rooms and counting the heads of the teachers.

The governments should realise that it should not try to micromanage and control any system even before it has taken its roots. What our private universities require is real autonomy. Politicians are nervous that these private institutions will become places of profiteering and extortion, if they are not properly bridled. The right to decide fees, intake of students etc. are must for the healthy growth of the educational institutions. It should be left to the competition and the market forces to decide the fees and not to a group of bureaucrats. If in the nascent stage these Universities do not boldly raise these issues they will do disservice to the future generations of students by providing them sub-standard education which only meets the external norms fixed by the authorities.

31 May, 2018

Private Universities

MP Private University Regulatory Commission organised a day-long celebration of its tenth foundation day. It was a day of some very plain talking and meaningful deliberations. Cultural presentations by the students and honouring of the Universities, faculty members and students added colour to the event which I also attended.

The chairman of the Commission and his full team deserve congratulations. Such events will add to the confidence of the private universities and exhort them to achieve excellence. It must be clear to every discerning person that the future of the higher education in India is with the private universities, and in a span of next few decades it will become evident. Majority of public (government) universities will stagnate due to extremely inflexible procedures and other well known ailments. We should know that out of the top 10 Universities in the world seven are private.

Here I want to make two points which were, of course, touched upon yesterday. UGC rules and regulations are binding on private universities. In other words government of India regulates us through UGC. One of the major functions of the UGC is to give grants, as is explicit in its name. But while UGC wants its writ to run large in the private universities, it (or may be MHRD) is shying away from giving grants to them. It is also surprising to note that UGC gives its 90% grants to the institutions having only 6% students. If the government wants private institutions to shoulder responsibility of higher education in India then, it is incumbent on it to help them to achieve world class quality research. MPPURC may request the state government to take this issue with the Central Government and NITI Ayog.

The second issue is finance. The Dean of Admissions of Harvard University had to disclose recently in a trial before a federal court, their secret method of admission. One thing he disclosed was that they give admissions to the relatives of rich donors and for this they use their discretion through a vague rating system. Can we have some flexibility here in admission system in private universities without jeopardising the interests of the ordinary students?

18 November, 2017

Visit to IIT Kharagpur

I visited IIT Kharagpur- the oldest IIT in India. This IIT was inaugurated by Maulana Azad on 18th August, 1951 in an imposing building which has a very interesting past. For its expansion, large number of other buildings have been added in the large campus of this institute.

This main building was made in 1909 for the DM office but was never used for this purpose. 1930 onward, it was used as a jail for lodging the revolutionaries and great political leaders. Here they suffered many atrocities and some were even killed in the firing. Later during World War II, this was used as American Air Base.

Now IIT has expanded in large number of buildings and its original building is converted into a museum of Science and Technology. Presently ten thousand students are studying here. There are one thousand teachers and over three thousand other staff. I visited class rooms, laboratories, books and digital libraries. Wide variety of subjects, including Environment is taught here. This institute has given to the nation a large number of eminent scientists, engineers, thinkers and leaders in many fields.

The existence of this IIT is a tribute to the Nehruvian vision of new India.

11 January, 2018

Lucknow University

I reached Lucknow. There I also passed through my fond Alma Mater, Lucknow University and took a pictue. In front of this gate, a big Metro station has come up. I feel proud of being its alumni.

The idea of starting a University at Lucknow was first mooted by Raja Sir Mohammad Ali Mohammad Khan, of Mahmudabad. A little later Sir Harcourt Butler was appointed Lieutenant-Governor of the United Provinces, and his well- known interest in all matters under his jurisdiction, especially in matters educational, gave fresh life and vigour to the proposal. In the meeting of General Committee of educationists Sir Harcourt Butler, who was in the chair, outlined the proposed scheme for the new university in 1919. Next year, the university is looking for its centenary.

I remember good old days I spent here in early seventies in free flowing camaraderie of youth. It was also a period of eruption of a volcano of thoughts and ideas in me, which has still not become dormant.

29 November, 2019

Educating Children-NEP 2020

In a bold move, Modi government has announced a new education policy (NEP 2020). It has come 34 years after Rajiv Gandhi last announced his policy of education. At that time, the basic focus of the policy was to equalise the opportunities for education, especially for SC/ST and women. It has achieved its objectives but failed to improve the quality of education.

The present policy includes school as well as higher education, but here my concern is with the school education. The objectives of policy for school education are very ambitious keeping in view the requirements of the 21st century. Let us see the salient features of this policy for school education. NEP has rightly emphasised to inculcate critical thinking among children instead of old system of rote learning. It has focused on age between three and six for preschool, as it is the crucial time for the development of cognitive power of children. Consequently, this policy aims to impart basic literacy and mathematical skills by the time the child enters 3rd Grade. At secondary school curriculum, there is no strict segregation of arts, science and commerce, and there is flexibility of options. Most importantly, there is integration of vocational training at the school level so that there is no stigma attached to such training.

NEP has separated government role into two bodies, one that regulates education and second that runs public (government) schools. At present the same body regulates all schools and also runs the public schools. This body also regulates the private schools. Now a separate regulatory body will be giving directions to both public and private schools, and a separate body will run the public schools.

While the goals of NEP are very lofty, we have to see the hard realities. India has miserably failed in providing quality education in its public schools, where mostly poor children take admissions. No person of means, policy-maker or bureaucrat send their children to public schools. Due to very low quality of education in public schools, even the poor people are now sending their children both in urban and rural areas to cheap private schools. Surprisingly, now nearly half the students of India are in private schools. Yet, in spite of some very expensive private schools, the average spending of private schools is only one-third of public schools. Thus, taxpayers' money is being wasted in public schools with high expenditures and very low outcomes. What is the problem with public schools? Out of four public school teachers, one is always absent and half of those who are present do not teach. In many states, less than 10% teachers have passed teacher eligibility test. It is no wonder that less than half the students in class five can read a paragraph from text or do math sum from class two! There is an international test called PISA for testing science, reading and arithmetic skills of school children. Sadly, in this test India came 73rd out of 74 participating countries. It was so embarrassing to UPA government that they stopped this test. The root cause of this dismal picture in public schools is the total absence of any accountability of teachers whatsoever. There is no political will to enforce the teachers' accountability.

As a result of this rot in public schools, even the very poor people are shifting their children to private schools. Large numbers of private schools have come up in urban slums and rural areas and some of them provide education for even less than Rs 500 per month. These poor children's private schools are only a shade better than public schools but they try to teach English. All state governments, which have failed to run their own schools properly, are very keen for controlling the private schools. The biggest hypocrisy in India for both school and higher education is that the private educational institutions are supposed to be non-profit. The indifferent bureaucracy in various states requires from 35 to 125 permissions for opening a school. This leads to large scale corruption and fudging of accounts by private institutions. Policy makers have no issues with this hypocrisy. Out of 10 top economies of the world, India is the only economy which doesn't allow schools for profit but allows manipulation and open corruption.

What is the practical solution for improving the situation? Many educationists and economists have proposed to directly fund children. I fully agree with this view. Atal Bihari Vajpayee was thinking to introduce this idea. To be fair to the taxpayers who pay their hard earned money for non-productive public education, we may consider giving poor families vouchers with reasonable amount for funding their children for education. The public schools may coexist but only in competition with the private schools. Unless such constructive actions are taken and educational institutions are allowed to earn honest profit, and black money and corruption are eliminated, we will not achieve the cherished goals of NEP 2020. There can be no world class higher education without a solid foundation of the schools.

20 September, 2020

Induction Speech for Doctors

I, as Vice Chancellor, gave an induction address online to Doctors, who have joined as students of MD / MS in Index Medical College of my Malwanchal University. Covid-19 has taught us to explore technological options to overcome the social hindrance.

I advised the Doctors to develop a critical thinking and not to go for rote learning. They should mentally become agile to face any volatility or disruption in future. They should go for all round development of their personality and become a good doctor, as well as, a good human being.

25 August, 2020

On the Great Wall of China

Historic Site of the Battle of Plassey, West Bengal